FOREX TRADING:

Description

The trading market has no "one-size-fits-all" key. Some traders think they can simply purchase Forex trading programs and similar to an ATM- all that they have to do is input a PIN and they get all their cash. No, this is not how it works. This is an actual market, and it is the biggest financial market worldwide, so you have to regard it like that.

It is your decision if you want to be a part-time trader or you want to do it every day. You can even decide to make it a business - your trading business. If there is any secret actually, it is within your brain, and together with your mental awareness, control and accumulated skills and knowledge that you have acquired and the accordant alignment of your objectives and actions, and expertise that is gained through a quality amount of constant practice till knowledge becomes instinctive wisdom.

It is possible to learn to trade, however, the experience has to be acquired. It is developed personally through individual effort and comprehension. It does not just happen in one day. Like any other profession, trading also requires commitment. The theory is acceptable, but practice perfects your skills and combines all your previously acquired knowledge. One other important thing is to know that it is impossible to stop learning. Every day, there is a change in the market, and the Forex market like its traders, is constantly evolving.

What you put in is what you would get. Certainly, you have to invest in your learning, you have to search for knowledge and someone that can guide you through trading in this market. I believe that after you have read the book, it would not be hard for you to decide that you want me to guide teach you more.

This book gives a comprehensive guide on the following:

- Forex Trading Basics
- Elements Of Forex
- Forex Trading On A Budget
- The Position Trading Strategy
- Developing Your Trading Plan
- Think Before You Trade
- Trading Strategies
- Fundamental Analysis
- Trading Journals
- Engulfing Pattern Trading With 3ms Principles

- Psychology Of Forex Trading
- Tips For Success
- FAQs On Forex Trading... AND MORE!!!

The zeal to learn a minimum of one new thing every day is very crucial. After all these years, I still experience my own "Ah-ha" moments of awareness and I hope it never ends. However, these experiences have to be acquired personally. A few of them will be regarded as intuitive, and apparent to a lot of people, while for other people, they are unable to fully comprehend this.

Introduction

What is Forex?

The term *forex,* or also known as *foreign exchange,* *currency trading*, or simply *FX*, refers to the activity of trading the world's currencies. Trading currencies is important for business and foreign trade. This is what keeps businesses, as well as the world's different currencies in existence. For example, if you are an American tourist and you visit Egypt, you cannot pay the stores in USD as it is not the local currency that is accepted in Egypt. Instead, what you need to do is to exchange your USD for the local currency in Egypt, which is the Egyptian pound at its current exchange rate. Here is another example: Let us say that you live in the US and you want to buy a certain commodity from India, you will need to pay the Indian merchant in Indian rupees. Also, in order for the merchant to acquire the said commodity, then he will also have to pay in Indian rupees if he is buying it within India. However, if the Indian merchant is also going to import the said commodity, then he will have to convert his currency into the acceptable local currency of the seller. This constant need to exchange one currency for another makes the FX market the largest and most liquid financial market in the world.

Forex is also an excellent way to make a profit. As the most liquid financial market, there is a high potential to make a positive profit by trading currencies. In fact, there are professional traders out there who make a living solely from this activity. So, just how much can you make by trading currencies? You can make a few dollars up to thousands and even millions of dollars every month. The amount you can profit depends on your invested capital, as well as the outcome of a trade. It is worth noting that forex is also a type of investment. Hence, just like any other kind of investment, there is also the possibility of losing all your money. The good news is that there are things that you can do and strategies that you can apply that can significantly increase your chances of making a profit. These will be discussed in more detail later in the book. For now, you should first have a good foundation and understanding of what forex is all about.

The Forex Market

The forex market is the place where currencies are traded. So, where is this forex market located? One thing that you should understand is that the forex market is a decentralized market. What this means is that there is no central marketplace where forex is conducted. It does not have a physical place or location. Instead, it is made electronically online across a network of computers around the world. Therefore, if you want to trade cryptocurrency, you only have to use the Internet in order to access the forex market. As for the schedule, you have to consider that the forex market has a worldwide scope and that different countries can have different timezones. The forex market is open round the clock starting from Sunday at 5pm EST up to Friday at 4pm EST. The forex market is a continuously moving market, so you can expect to see how the price quotes of the different currencies change at any time of the day or night.

The forex market has two levels: the interbank market and the over-the-counter market (OTC). The interbank market is where banks trade. The OTC market is where regular traders engage in the FX activity. This is where you will trade using an online platform. Before you can trade currencies online, you will have to make an account with an FX broker. It is your broker who will provide you with the platform that you can use for trading.

Among the different types of currencies, the US dollar is the most traded currency. It comprises more than 80% of all trades. It is followed by the Euro, and then by the Japanese Yen.

The forex market is the most active market in the whole world, which makes it a highly profitable place for professional traders. However, you should keep in mind that it is also a challenging place. It is not a secret that there are a number of investors who have lost a big amount of their invested capital in just a few days; worse, some of them have lost all their invested money. Still, for those who understand what they are doing and give it enough focus, effort, and practice, the forex market is the perfect place where you can continuously rake in serious profits.

Is it for you? Although you are welcome to join and participate in the forex market, it does not always mean that it is also the place that will make you earn money. When you trade foreign currencies, there is only one of two possible outcomes: either you make money or lose it. The unfortunate truth is that not everyone can have success in the forex market. If you are the type who just wants to gamble and rely on luck, if you do not want to take time and efforts to study the market, then you will most likely lose your money in just a few days. However, if you are willing to exert serious efforts, if you can sit for hours and study what is going on in the forex market and make analysis, then you can significantly increase your chances of making a profit. Also, if you get really good at it, then you might even be able to turn the forex market into a path that leads financial freedom.

Forex Pairs

When you trade in the stock market, you need to understand forex pairs. They are composed of currencies that are being traded. The major currency pairs are the most liquid in the market, and they are the following: EUR/USD, GBP/USD, USD/JPY, USD/CHF, USD/CAD, and AUD/USD.

There are also currencies that are not traded with the US dollar, and so their pairs are considered as minor currency pairs. Although they are also considered as liquid, they are notas liquid as the major currency pairs.

The minor currencies include the GBP/JPY, EUR/GBP, and EUR/CHF.

As a forex trader, you need to understand how to read forex pairs. Take note that a forex pair involves two different currencies, for example: EUR/USD. Every currency pair is composed of a *base currency* and a *quote currency*. The base currency, also known as the *bid price*, refers to the first currency in a pair; and the second currency, also known as the *ask* price, is the second currency in a pair. Therefore, in our example (EUR/USD), the base currency is the EUR while the quote currency is the USD.

When you trade currencies, you will see a number after pair. For example, you may see something like this: EUR/USD 1.25. Take note that the base currency, which in this case is the EUR, is always equals to 1. Hence, you can view it as EUR 1/USD 1.25. What this simply means is that 1 EUR is equivalent to 1.25 USD.

What if you want to use USD as the base currency? In forex convention, it will then look like this, USD/EUR 0.80. Be careful not to just switch the two currencies and their values. Instead, you have to divide the base currency by the quote currency. Although they may seem different, their mathematical relation remains the same. If you divide 1 by 0.80, you will get back to the value of 1.25.

Ask and Bid

Now that you have a better understanding of a forex currency pair, it is time to understand the two important things about a forex quote: The ask and bid price. Let us use an example:

EUR/USD = 1.3400/07

In a normal situation, the difference between the ask and bid price is just a very small amount, usually less than 1/100th of a unit, it has become a normal part of a forex convention to just show the last two digits. In this case, it is 07. If you write this down in its complete form, it will look like this: EUR/USD = 1.34000/1.3407.

Here is something that you need to realize: The bid price does not refer to the price that you need to bid in order to purchase a currency pair. The bid and ask price should be taken from the perspective of your forex broker. Therefore, in order to make a profit from a transaction, a broker will *ask* higher than the price that he would be willing to *bid* if you were the one selling the currency pair. In our example, since you want to buy the EUR which refers to the base currency, then you will have to pay the *ask* price of the broker which is 1.3407 USD. If you are the one who is selling, then you need to accept your broker's bid of 1.3400. AS you can see, either way, it is in favor of your broker. Now, the difference between the ask price and the bid price is what is referred to as the *spread*. Obviously, it is the commission that your broker receives from a trade.

Forex: Buy and selling

What does it mean to buy and sell currencies in the forex market? Forex is about trading currencies, and it is participated by banks and individuals worldwide. When a trade is made in the forex market, there are always two sides to it: there is someone who buys a currency in a pair, and there is another who sells the other currency in a pair. As an FX trader, you make a profit by predicting whether the value of a currency in a pair will increase or decrease against the value of another currency. For example, let us say that you buy US$5,000 by selling $4,000 euros. In this example, the position that you have is that you predict that the value of the US dollar will appreciate (increase) against the euro. If your prediction is correct, then you will make a profit. Now, in order to realize your profit, you still need to sell your US dollars. In this case, you should sell your US$5,000 into euro. In exchange, you will then receive more than $4,000 euros. Needless to say, the value of US dollar must first increase against the euro before you sell them. As you can see, buying and selling foreign currencies is simple and easy to do. You just have to predict if the value of a currency will increase or decrease against the value of the other currency in a pair.

Percentage in Point

Percentage in point, simply referred to as simply *pip*. This refers to the measure of a *spread*. Take note that the spread refers to the difference between the bid price and the ask price and is the commission that your broker receives. The pip is the change in value the value of a particular currency. You might have heard some traders who say that they want to profit by 500 pips. So, what does a pip exactly mean? To illustrate, let us say that the price of a currency pair changes from 1.6000 to 1.6001, then that is a change by 1 pip. Hence, a pip is a unit of value that is used to show the change in the value of a currency pair. It is important to understand the pip because it signifies how much you can profit or lose. For example, if a trader buys the currency pair EUR/USD, he will profit if the price of EUR increases relative to the USD. To illustrate: Let us say that you buy in the pair EUR/USD, you buy the EUR for $1.7500. If you exit the trade at $1.7600, then that is a profit by 100 pips. Of course, if the value decreases, then the value of the pips would be on the negative, say -100 pips, and that signifies a loss.

So, how many pips should you aim for? There is no hard and fast rule as to the number of pips that you should gain. Of course, the longer you hold on to a currency pair the more significant the pip value may change since the price of the different currencies fluctuates slowly. Of course, there is also the possibility that their prices will go back to their original price, depending on their price movement. For small trades, many are already contented with 50 pips or even 30 pips. The key is to be on a positive profit.

Types of Orders

There are different orders that you can give to your broker as to how you want to trade currencies. These orders may be used to control how you enter and exit the FX market. Hence, they play an important element in building a successful career as a foreign currency trader.

- Market order

A market order is the most common type of order in forex. This order tells the broker to buy or sell a currency pair at the best possible price. This happens instantly and is always executed by the broker. A market order is the best way to enter the market as quickly as possible.

- Entry order

As the name implies, an entry order is a way to enter the market. It is difficult to spend the whole day monitoring the market just to see when you will enter it. In this case, you can just use an entry order and be able to spend your time away from the computer. In an entry order, you get to enter the market once the price reaches a certain point.

- Limit order

A limit order is often used to exit a market at a profit. This order directs your broker to buy or sell a specific number of units of a currency pair at a defined value. If you have a long position, then the limit order should be higher than the current market price. If you are taking a short position, then the limit order would be lower than the market price. This of it as a limiting line where you trade will be automatically closed once it reaches that line. Of course, once this line is reached, then you will receive whatever profit you may have into your account balance.

- Stop order

A stop order is used to exit a trade. It is also referred to as *stop-loss order*. The purpose of this order is to control or limit the possible losses that you may experience. Hence, it closes a trade that reaches a certain level of loss. Although a stop order is not a good sign when its defined limit is reached, it is able to limit your losses and closes a trade in order to prevent you from losing more.

Risk/Reward Ratio

The risk/reward ratio simply refers to the calculation of how much you should risk in a trade as compared to how much you should profit from it. For example, if you are making a trade and you set a stop loss at 15 pips and then set your take-in profit at 25 pips, then your risk reward ratio will be 15:25. This means that you are risking 15 pips in order to earn 25 pips.

When used in Forex, the key is to look for an opportunity where you reward will be much higher than the risk. It will be great if you always find trades where the reward always outweighs the risk but such is not always the case. Although it is commonly advised that a high reward and low risk trade is the most ideal, the contrary may be practical when you notice that the market is highly volatile. There is no strict rule as to the most ideal risk reward ratio should be. It may depend on the type of trader that you are, as well as the trading strategy that you use. Of course, as a professional trader, it is still ideal to make more trades where the reward is much higher than the risk in order to increase your chances of ending up with a positive profit after you sum up all your winnings and losses.

Leverage

One of the reasons why many people like to engage in forex is because it gives them a higher leverage unlike other financial instruments. But what does the term *leverage* mean? A leverage allows you to borrow money that you can invest from your broker. Since you will be able to borrow money, you will be able to invest a higher amount, which means that you will have a higher potential profit since you will be earning a certain percentage of your investment. Forex is known for offering a high leverage, which means that for an initial margin, you can be trading a big amount of money. The leverage can vary from50:1, 100:1, or even 200:1, depending on your broker and the size of your position. Take note that before you can start engaging in forex, you should first open an account with your broker; in this case, you need a margin account. So, what do these leverages mean? A 50:1 leverage signifies that the minimum margin requirement is only 2% (1/50) of the total value of trade in his trading account available as cash. Accordingly, a 1:100 leverage would only require 1%, and so on. The usual leverages used as 1:50 and 1:100. A leverage of 1:200 is used normally for positions that are around $50,000 or less.

In application, what this means is that if you want to trade $100,000 with a 1% margin (100:1 leverage), then you only need to invest $1,000 in your margin account. Obviously, this leverage is so much higher than the 2:1

leverage that you get when you put your money in equities or the 15:1 leverage when you invest in futures market. Now, although a leverage of 100:1 may seem very high and risky, do not forget that foreign currencies do not fluctuate so high in one trading day. Normally, they only fluctuate by less than 1% in a trading day.

An obvious advantage of leveraging is that it allows you to have a decent trading size even if you only have a substantial investment capital to begin with. Many professional traders recommend at a minimum of $1,000 as an initial capital for forex. However, the problem is that not all traders can afford to risk a thousand dollars. Also, risking $1,000 when you are just a beginner might not be the best choice to make. This is where leveraging comes into play.

*But, can you still trade foreign currencies without leveraging?*The answer, of course, is in the affirmative. There are some notable traders who do not leverage their position. Here is an example of how *not* leveraging can be an advantage: Let us say that you purchase 1,000 USD using 800 EUR without any leverage. Let us assume that the price of USD experiences a 50% drop in price, then you will only lose only 50% or just 400 EUR. This means that you are still in the game. Now, consider the same example but let us assume that you are using 100:1 leverage' even if the price changes by less than 1%, then you will lose all your funds. Of course, an obvious disadvantage of not leveraging is that you will earn a much lower amount than you would normally have. After all, if you cannot expect to profit a very high percentage of your invested funds. Normally, a professional investor only makes a decent and reasonable percentage profit. Hence, the bigger your fund is, the more money you can make.

What is a Lot?

A *lot* refers to the smallest size that you can trade in the forex market. Hence, it also has to do with your risk exposure. As a trader, you should find the best lot size that is suitable for you based on your current trading account. The lot size can also have an impact how much you will be affected by the forex market movement. For example, if you only have a small trade, a 100-pip movement would not be too significant. However, if you are holding a huge lot, a 100-pip movement can have a strong impact. In your career as a trader, you will surely encounter different lot sizes. As already stated, it is important that you understand them so that you will know which lot size is suitable for you:

- Micro lot

As the name already implies, this is usually the smallest lot that is offered by most brokers. A micro lot refers to a lot of 1,000 units of a currency that your account is funded with. Hence, if you are using US dollars, then a micro lot is equivalent to $1,000 USD. If you want to trade a pair that is dollar-based, then 1 pip is equivalent to 10 cents. If you are a beginner, then it is advised that you stick to micro lots.

- Mini lots

A mini lot is equal to 10,000 units of the currency in your account. Hence, if you are trading an account that is dollar based, and if you are trading a pair that is also dollar-based, then a single pip in a trade will be equal to $1. Compare this with a micro lot where 1 pip is only 10 cents. It should also be noted that in forex trading, the market can move by more than a hundred pips per day. So, just imagine how much profit or losses you can experience. Obviously, trading mini lots requires a higher capital than trading micro lots.

- Standard lots

A standard lot is 100,000 units of the currency of your funding account. If you are trading in US dollars, that is equal to $100,000 USD. Hence, the average pip size for a standard lot is equal to $10 a pip. Therefore, when it says that you are up by 10 pips, then that is equivalent to $100 profit. However, in the case of losing 10 pips, then that would translate to $100 loss. To make trades using standard lots, you should have at least $25,000 as standard lots are mostly for large accounts. Most traders only trade using micro lots and sometimes mini lots.

Chapter 1 Forex Trading Basics

While the concept of forex trading is easy, executing your trades in the market is difficult. This doesn't mean you won't become successful. What it means is that you will need to educate yourself and work hard. The first step anyone should take is to learn as much as possible about forex trading.

Understanding Pairs

The main difference between the stock market and the forex market is that, in forex, you are essentially trading pairs of currency (that is you buy one currency and sell another), while in the stock market, you buy shares of a company. This is not an option when you are forex trading. Whether you are trading, selling, or buying, you have to use pairs. For example, the Japanese yen is often paired against the Canadian dollar and the Euro against the American dollar.

What's a Pip?

A pip is a 1% movement in the currency value. A pip is a basic unit that is used when talking about currency quotes. It is the last number of the quote, so when you are following the movement of two currencies, you observe from the last two digits so that you can say that a currency moved by the number of pips that differentiates the second from the starting figure. The value of the pip is determined from the size of the trade. You make a decision to buy or sell a currency pair depending on your estimation, which is when you make the market order.

Entry Order

When you use an entry order, you enter your currency pair trade at a specific price. If the price of the currency never reaches the specific price, then your trade is not enforced. If the price is reached, then your trade is completed regardless of your presence at the time.

Stop-Loss Order

A stop-loss order is the price at which you want your dealer to exit the trade when the trade moves against your interests. A stop-loss order prevents losses.

Limit

A limit is the price at which you want the dealer to exit the trade when it's moving in your favor. Knowing when to exit the trade even when things are looking up is useful because you can hardly predict when a currency will start to drop.

Margin

When you are buying or selling at a good margin, that means that you control a large amount of currency for an initial investment that is way smaller in comparison. For example, a 100-by-1 margin means that you invest $1,000 for a trade of $100,000. Buying and selling on a margin is safe and appealing because the only amount you risk to lose is the amount you invested, but you have the opportunity to profit a greater amount.

Leveraging Ratios

You are betting at leveraging ratios. A $1,000 bet on 1,000 value of the currency is considered 1:1 leverage.

Trading platforms allow you to follow and market currency in a way that creates a profit. When you're successful in trading one currency so that its value increases against the currency you used to buy it, you can make a profit. You are speculating whether the currency will rise or drop. Your chances of profiting essentially increase with the success of your predictions.

With forex, you trade using leverage, which means that you only need to invest a portion of your positions. By using stop-losses, you can prevent losing your investment.

When it comes to currency rates, many factors have an influence. Interest rates, unemployment numbers, political events, and many more affect the country's currency value.

Currencies may rise and fall in different values for different reasons, one of them being large companies exchanging currencies for the purpose of international trading. The time and circulation of market information is also a significant factor. False and accurate information circulating the market can influence banks to swiftly market currencies, which additionally affects the changes in currency values.

Diversification

You want to ensure you have diversity within your portfolio to tackle risk. In fact, because the forex market is open 24 hours a day during the weekdays, the market holds more diversity. Therefore, don't just focus on the popular currencies, such as the American dollar and Canadian dollar. You may also trade other pairs such as

American dollar/British pound (USD/GBP) or American dollar/Japanese Yen (USD/JPY).

What Are The Risks?

While there are many people trading in forex, there are also those who are facing major financial losses. Since forex trading is essentially all about predictions, one of the biggest risks, obviously, is making a wrong prediction. The following are the many risks of forex trading.

The Wrong Mindset

When it comes to any market, you always need to have the right mindset. Take a moment to think about how certain emotions, such as fear or worry, can control your thoughts. You have to find a way to keep your emotions out of the market. Experienced traders call the right mindset the winning mindset. The following are some key characteristics that will help you gain your winning attitude.

1. *You need to be self-disciplined.* You want to make sure that you take all the steps to ensure you are doing what you need to do to reach success. This means that you complete daily

research to see how the forex market is doing, and you document all your currencies, trades, and any other information. Fortunately, most marketing platforms keep your information in its history. However, it is always best that you find a way to keep the files on your computer so that you always have them. You follow any rules and guidelines that your mentor or yourself have set up.

2. *You are also able to keep your emotions in check.* This might mean that you follow certain strategies you set up for yourself, such as deep-breathing exercises. You don't allow yourself to give in to your excitement if a trade goes well or when you see your account balance. While you might smile and be proud of yourself, you don't allow the feeling to take over as you can become too confident. This can lead you to make mistakes, which can put you and your finances in jeopardy.

3. *You understand that mistakes are going to be made.* Instead of focusing on your mistakes and allowing them to control your future decisions, you learn from them. Many traders write down their mistakes in their trading journal or daily reports.

4. *You understand that the market is fluid and are able to adjust to the changes.* For instance, if a price notes that you need to make a change in your portfolio, then you make a change. Your portfolio is the place where you keep all the currencies that you can sell or trade.

5. *You understand your risk tolerance.* No matter what strategies you use to try to limit your risk, there is always a risk. If you aren't comfortable with a lot of risks, you will want to focus more on trades that are low risk.

Currency-Value Fluctuations

There are internal-market reasons and external reasons for a currency's value changes. Internally, one country's currency can increase while another currency you hold decreases. These fluctuations are often dependent on how many people are buying and selling the currency. For example, if the yen isn't strong, then more people will purchase the yen, which makes the value increase. This could show a decrease in the American dollar in comparison to the yen because traders are using the American dollar to purchase yen. In other words, the more people purchase currency, the stronger its value. The more people sell a currency, the lower its value.

External factors can be anything from politics to other events going on within the country. These are factors that traders cannot control but you should always be aware of. Because of this, many traders will spend at least half an hour every morning going through the news in order to get an idea of what the market is going to look like that day. Doing this will allow you to know if you should purchase a currency or trade one within your portfolio.

Broker Risk

While not every trader has a broker, it is important for a beginner to look into a broker. This person can help you learn about the market and give you advice on what moves to take. However, there are broker risks. In order to limit these risks, you want to ensure you can trust your broker. Do some research before you decide to take on a broker. The best way you can do this is by choosing a broker who is part of a government body as it is regulated. Government bodies have to follow guidelines and ethics.

How To Start

Whenever you start trading, you want to ensure you follow certain steps for success.

First, you always want to do your research. You want to learn as much as possible. This means you will read books, join forex trading forums, find a trusted broker, and anything else you feel is necessary. Once you feel like you know forex trading like the back of your hand, you will be able to move on.

Second, ensure you understand the language. Forex trading has its own language. Take your time to learn these terms, and if you have questions, find another trader to discuss your concerns with.

Third, you want to find your trusted broker. This person will help you make decisions and explain the world of investing to you. Take your time to find the best broker for you. Your broker will help you set up an account.

Fourth, take time to analyze the forex market. Learn about the charts and what they mean. Look back in the history of some currencies so you can gain a better understanding of trading. For example, charts can help you analyze the best time for trading and which currencies are best within the market and help you find the best currencies.

Fifth, if you are trading full-time, set up an office and your schedule. You want to find time to ensure you are self-disciplined enough that you won't struggle with distractions. Take the time to set a start date.

Sixth, once your day arrives, start trading. Make sure that you go through your morning routine, such as reading the paper and seeing how the currencies are doing. Notice any changes that occurred overnight. You also want to ensure you go through your daily schedule and close out your day with your evening routine. For example, check your stocks for the day, and discuss anything about your day in your journal.

How To Profit

Once you start trading, you will want to do what you can to limit your risks. While you will always have some risk, you can find a comfortable level of risk. Another way to profit is by diversifying your portfolio. This means that you will have different currencies and not focus on the same ones.

You also want to be patient. Forex trading is not a get-rich-quick scheme. It will take time to start seeing a profit. Don't give up, and don't fall into the wrong mindset. If you need any help, talk to your broker, a mentor, or someone in the forum. There are many experienced forex traders who are happy to help beginners.

Continue to communicate with your broker, mentor, and anyone on the forum. Even if you spend months researching, people will always be important when it comes to your success. Don't allow yourself to get into the mindset that you know everything. Continue to learn as much as possible. Take time to practice analyzing reports. You have to do whatever you need to so you feel comfortable as a trader.

Chapter 2 Elements Of Forex

Before you get started on your first trading in the forex market, take a moment to think about how you want to approach your trades. There is more to the forex market and currency trading than what is instantly obvious, and I believe the way you trade is one of the essential elements of your trading success.

Your success typically comes in the form of a trading plan. With your plan, you get to decide how, when, and why you would like to make a certain trade, establish rules, or manage expectations. It is sort of like your own trading signature that you use to make your decisions.

In this chapter, I will help you consider the focal points of trading as you outline your own method of trading currencies. Once we accomplish that, we can review the features of some of the most frequently used trading methods. Then we go through the process of developing your trading plan.

We will also focus on technical analysis, helping you understand how to read the market. Then we can focus on making sure that you do not miss out on opportunities as much as possible. Finally, we can evaluate the methods by which you can manage risks.

All the above steps help you slowly acclimate yourself to the forex market.

But first, what exactly is a trading style?

Your trading style dictates when you would like to make a specific trade, the frequency of your trades, and what you expect your profit margins to be on a particular day.

So how do you develop your own styles? By creating an effective plan.

Arm Yourself! Creating A Trading Plan

You need a systematized trading plan for yourself, or you won't succeed much in the markets. The distinction between making and losing money when dealing with currencies can be as simple as trading with a plan or trading without one. A trading plan is an ordered approach to implementing a trade tactic that you have established based on your market outlook and analysis.

There are three components that I believe you have to ponder upon for your trading plan:

Finalizing Size of the Position

How big a position will you adopt for your trade strategy? A position simply refers to a particular transaction you are going to take or you have already taken. When you choose your position size, you can effectively decide how much money you are willing to invest in each trade.

Where to Begin Your Position

At what point will you try to open your preferred position? What happens if you do not reach the level you aimed for during your entry?

Setting Stop-Loss and Take-Profit Levels

You have to decide where you would like to exit the position, both when you have a winning hand (take profit) and when you have a losing trade (stop-loss). Your exit strategy allows you to determine your plan for the next position whenever you decide to start it.

That is all there is to it; you just need three fundamental elements. However, you will be surprised to know how many traders (both beginners and veterans) end up opening positions without having prepared a thorough game plan. There are more points to consider when preparing your trading plan, but for now, I want to place emphasis on the point that trading without a systematized plan is like navigating in a dark cave with your blindfold on and with no draft of air to guide you. Where are you planning to go without a proper guide?

Also, it does not matter how well thought out your trading plan is; it is not going to be effective if you are not following it. You might say, "Well, isn't that obvious, Mr. Author?" Actually no. Numerous traders are excited about developing a plan only to toss it all aside when they become impulsive. They face an influx of emotions, which only tends to distract them and their well-crafted plans.

Sometimes, an unforeseen piece of information or news causes traders to let go of their trade plan midway without even considering what their actions are going to cause.

When someone abandons his or her plan, it is as good as never having created a trading plan at all.

Forming a trading plan and making sure that you adhere to it are the two main components of trading with currencies. If I had to narrow down and let you know which is the most important characteristic of a good trader, then it would not be his or her skills in using technical analysis, the experience accumulated, or even the tenaciousness—though they are all vital. It would be his or her discipline. You see, if you can practice discipline, then you can learn the other skills and requirements easily.

Traders who stick to a disciplined attitude are the ones who endure for years and make the most profits from their trades. It does not make them perfect—far from it. They are still capable of making numerous mistakes. However, it is their discipline that allows them to recover faster and get back into the trade, eventually netting them profits and recovering their losses.

Expect Your Expectations

When you are trading in currencies as a beginner, then you have a whole lot of expectations on your trade. This is understandable since new traders do not have a history they can rely on as a reference. They are still unfamiliar with price shifts and currency movements. They often think about how much they can make in a single trade.

That is not an easy question to answer and, quite frankly, not a question to think about when you are just starting out.

You have to understand this vital point—the forex market is not an ATM. You cannot simply deposit money into it and then withdraw that money whenever you feel like it (well, you can actually, but that does not mean you get back what you had invested). There are a multitude of traders speculating on the direction that various currency pairs are going to take; some of those traders are going to make the right speculation and earn a profit, and some of them are going to be wrong and not earn profits. In some case, traders might be right for a certain period before ending up on the wrong side of their prediction.

Ways to Trade

You need to understand that you have numerous ways to engage with your trade. Not all of them might be suited for you. What you need to do is practice with various techniques. After that, narrow down the trading style that best fits your requirement. Once you are able to do that, you can ensure that you are reading data before making any decision.

Short-Term Trading

There is a fundamental difference in the way we trade in currencies in the short term as opposed to other forms of securities. If you have ever been in the stock market, then you know that you cannot simply buy and sell a stock at a time of your convenience. This means that you cannot purchase a stock and then decide to sell it at the end of the day. But with the currency market, the situation is completely different. This is because you get to deal with a market that fluctuates in small increments quite frequently. When you are dealing with pips, you are dealing with an extremely small point change (imagine 0.0001 jump or dive in a currency).

This is why, in a short-term forex trading, you can strategize your sale in such a way that you do not have to keep your trades with you for longer than an hour. That could benefit those who do not have a lot of time to spend on their trades in a given day or those who prefer quick trades and small gains over time. However, the time factor is not the most appealing of all factors in short-term trading. The thing that really attracts traders to this style of trading is the small pip changes. Traders who indulge in short-term trading create profits by frequently opening and closing positions after seeing an increase in just a few pips, sometimes even as little as 1 or 2 pips.

An interbank market is a network where financial institutions interact with each other in order to trade in currencies. In their world, when someone (or an entity) deals with extremely short-term trades, where they are opening and closing positions quickly, then that particular trading is called as "jobbing" the market. Online currency traders, on the other hand, have another name for it—scalping. You can call it whatever you like, either jobbing or scalping, both terms can work. Traders who engage in this style of trading are considered to be some of the most attentive and focused traders. This is because they have to make quick-second decisions for their trade.

If you want to be a successful scalper, then do not stick to a particular position. You should not worry about the up and down movement of the currency. What you are focused on is the pips. That is what will get you the returns you seek. If the position you have chosen is not working for you, then make a quick exit. Look for volatility and liquidity of the currency as your prime factors.

Here are a few tips for short-term trading:

1. Make sure you are focusing on high liquid pairs, such as USD/JPY, EUR/USD, EUR/JPY, EUR/GBP, and EUR/CHF. The pairs that are the most liquid have the smallest-sized trading spreads and fewer sudden price leaps.

2. And what exactly is a spread? Well, in the world of forex trading, you have to deal with two terms, "ask" and "bid." The price that is quoted for selling a particular currency pair is termed as "ask" while the price that is quoted to a trader for the purchase of a currency pair is called "bid." The difference between them is called a spread. So in this case, you do not want to have a big gap with the ASK and BID, or you might not make a lot of profits.

3. Trade with just one currency pair at a time. Dealing with multiple currencies means having to deal with the risks, trends, and quick fluctuations of those currencies. When you are dealing with the price movements of currencies that happen every second or minute, you do not want to be distracted easily by different pairs. You might not only end up making mistakes but also not make a profit at all. Additionally, you also get to feel comfortable with the pair that you are dealing with.

4. Make sure you manage your risk and reward expectations. As each spread you receive will be different, you need to know that what you can earn from those spreads will be unique. Most major pairs have close to 2- to 5-pip spread, and you should be aiming to get a hold

of 3 to 10 pips per trade in order to negate any losses that the market might suddenly have.

5. Do not trade around the time that data releases. When the market releases some data, then there is usually a gap in the prices. This happens because the data is being added into the systems, and you might notice after a little while. This level of unpredictability might not suit the short-term trade strategy that you have set up. When you deal with currencies, you might notice that the markets receive price adjustments almost 15 to 20 minutes before the release of any major date. This could cause a sudden shift against your position that may not be solved before the data comes out.

Medium-Term Trading

In medium-term trading, you are holding a position for a period that extends from a few minutes to a few hours. Some people might extend that to more than just a few hours, but traders rarely hold the position for more than a day. Because of short periods involved in medium-term trading, you do not concern yourself with the length of time but the pips you are working with. And yes, this is quite similar to short-term trading as well.

However, short-term trading does not deal with the overall position of the market. Its main concern is the profit that it can make from small price fluctuations. On the other hand, medium-term trading wants to focus on getting the general direction of the trade correct and make a profit from major currency movements.

Here are some tips for when you are using medium-term trading:

1. Keep your eyes attached to the news. You are going to need it! This is because you need to have at least a basic idea on the direction in which a currency pair is likely to shift. This means that while you are performing minute changes, you are vaguely aware of the overall situation, making use of the knowledge to your advantage.

2. You need to rely on technical analysis. This is important because you should base your market expectations on chart readings, trend lines, support and resistance levels, and momentum studies. When you utilize technical analysis, you may be able to locate an opportunity somewhere on your charts, but by empowering yourself with global events, you might be able to make informed decisions. This, in turn, helps you open positions comfortably.

3. When you know about events, you become informed about factors such as central bank events, interest rates, unemployment rate, and more. These factors help you predict the outcome of the position you are about to open, and they give some you ideas on when to make a closing.

Long-Term or Macroeconomic Trading

This form of trading is for those with deep pockets and plenty of moolah to spend. We are talking about hedge funds and multimillion-dollar (and even multi-billion) corporations. When traders and institutions deal with long-term strategies, they open positions for a period of weeks, sometimes even months. In some cases, the trade is held on to for years because the returns from those positions are incredibly massive. However, that does not mean long-term trading does not have its own set of flaws. For example, it has a high degree of probability of facing numerous short-term volatile situations.

Carry Trade Strategies

In a carry trade, you invest in currencies that generate high returns and then sell currencies that have a lower yield than the currency you bought. Traders can benefit from this strategy in a couple of ways:

By having a long position in a high-yielding currency and a short position in a low-yielding currency, you can earn the difference in the interest rates between the two currencies. This interest is commonly referred to as "carry." However, if you end up in the opposite position (when you have a long position in a low-yielding currency and a short position in a high-yielding currency), the rate of interest ends up working against you, and you end up in a loss that is termed as the "cost of carry." A carry trade, in short, is simply making use of the difference between currencies of two different yields.

Now one of the most important aspects to consider is that you should jump in on a trade when you hear or see news about central banks working on their interest rates. This is because more traders end up taking advantage of the margin between the two currencies to make a profit out of it.

Let us take an example to illustrate this point. Let us assume that a particular trader spots the fact that interest rates in Japan are currently set at 0.5%. In the United States, the interest rate is close to 5%. What does this mean? The trader is hoping to make a profit of 4.5%, which is the difference between the two rates. He will first borrow yen and change them to dollars. Next, he will search for securities to invest in that will pay him using the US rate. With that, he will be able to pay back what he borrowed and make a cool profit out of his transaction. Pretty neat, huh?

Of course, there is always a downside. In this case, you can chalk it out to market volatility. If the price of the yen improves, then the trader might end up getting lower profits. If the value keeps increasing, then the trader can effectively kiss his or her original plan goodbye. However, many traders take into account this risk and place their expected profits at a rate that is adjusted for any changes in the market. However, once again, you cannot always predict that the trader's plan will work. What if the market suddenly shifts even further?

Carry trades are best focused on when the market has low volatility. This is because you can expect the financial markets to remain stable and avoid massive shifts. Another thing to keep in mind is that you need to have a big-enough interest rate between the two currencies to make a significant amount of money. Ideally, I would recommend looking for at least an interest rate of 2%.

Chapter 3 Forex Trading On A Budget

If you have just started in Forex trading, you must have been wondering whether you need to have a huge amount of money in order to start trading. So, is it possible for you to trade the Forex market with little money?

The fact is that you can trade with little money, but your profits will be limited. With a few tips though, you can successfully trade the markets without having to put down thousands of dollars on the line.

Educate Yourself

Before you can place your money on the line, you need to be educated about what to do before you jump in. Make sure you understand the basics of trading the Forex market and know whether your limited funds will give you profit.

Understand the risk management processes as well as other concepts before you put any money on the line. If you have put some money on the line, then you should withdraw part of it and put it in a course. It will give you concepts that you can use to turn your money regardless of how much you have.

Learning resources also introduce you to analysis techniques that give you an idea of what trade to place and when to do it.

Start Small

As a new trader, it is prudent that you start off with a small amount compared to putting all your money into the trade. Remember that you can't have the success you desire trading dollars when you cannot trade for pennies. To do this, you need to find the right broker that gives you a low limit trading account.

Patience is Key

Forex trading is all about having patience. When you start small, you might see it be frustrating and slow, but it keeps you disciplined. Make sure that you start small and grow your account step by step.

Profitable Forex investing takes time and patience. All those traders that you see making money on the market were novices on their first day, some were even worse than you. However, most of them started small and grew step by step to become the pro traders that they are right now.

Do It Regularly

As you refine the craft, make sure you make trading your habit. To do this, start investing regularly as you learn the ropes. Add funds to your account several times a week and you will see the account grow. The good thing is that you won't lose too much in any trade compared to putting up a lot of your money for trading.

How to Earn With Forex

There Are A Few Steps To Make Money With Forex. Let Us Look At What You Can Do.

Grow Your Skills

When You Have The Right Skill, You Will Make Money With Forex Trading. The Forex Market Is Dynamic, And You Have To Keep Up With The Changes. As You Trade, You Get More And More Knowledgeable About The Things That Happen In Forex Trading. Take Time To Learn New Techniques And Engage With Other Traders To Understand What They Do To Be Successful.

The best way to learn about Forex trading is to make sure you look at the various reasons the market is moving in a specific direction. For instance, you might look at the analysis methods that are used by top traders and why they use them. You also need to understand what triggers make the prices to move in a given direction as opposed to another.

Learn to Perform Analysis

The analysis is all about using charts and other visual tools to come up with a decision. Forex trading gives you two major types of tools to use – fundamental and technical analysis. Fundamental analysis focuses on events that will change the performance of a currency pair. On the other hand, technical analysis involves looking at price action and its effect on the market – including the trends, momentum, and reversal patterns.

We shall look at these analysis methods in details later, but at the moment, just know that you have a chance to make more profit when you perform the right analysis before placing a trade.

Work with the Right Broker

A Forex broker makes it possible for you to execute transactions. This is just one of the major functions – a broker handles various other tasks that are vital to trading.

Before you can choose a broker, make sure that you understand what they offer in terms of features and look at the reviews that are left by previous traders. If you come across fraud alerts or issues with the withdrawing of funds, then look for another broker.

So, making money on Forex is all about buying a currency pair at a low price, and then selling it off at a higher price to make profits. The profit, which represents your income, is the difference between the price you buy the price of buying and selling the currency pair. You pay the broker a commission from the trade called the spread.

If you believe that you don't have the capacity to place trades with your money, then you can use a feature given by the broker called the leverage. This is money that you follow from the broker to make your deposit higher.

Remember that the higher the deposit the more the risk.

Advantages of Trading Forex

When you get into forex trading, you enjoy various benefits that come with the trades that you place.

Low Commission

The commission is the money that the broker makes on each trade that you place. Usually, when you trade in a different place, the broker takes a percentage of the money that you deposit to the account.

However, many brokers don't attach any fees on the trade, meaning that you can enjoy high-profit margins when you trade Forex.

Trading Flexibility

Forex gives you a lot of flexibility for both traders and investors. You don't have a limit to the amount you place on trade each day, which allows both smalltime traders as well as seasoned investors to make money.

Additionally, you don't have too many rules and regulations when it comes to Forex trading. This means you have the flexibility to work 24 hours without any disruption.

The flexible working hours make it possible for those people working day jobs to have some time to trade as well.

You have Complete Control over Your Trades

One of the top advantages of trading Forex is that you have total control when you place a trade. You don't have to run a trade that you are not comfortable with.

It is all upon you to decide when and how to place a trade without any obligation. You also decide the level of risk that you can take in every trade.

Demo Accounts Ideal for Practicing

As a rookie in the business, you need all the guidance and information to make it in the market. For you, a demo account is all you need to achieve the skills necessary to give you the push you need.

The demo account is a simulation of the way the live trading system works, and it gives you the practice you need.

When you use the demo account, you don't face any risk and it gives you an idea of whether the market is ideal for you or not. You also get to test, improve, and organize the new skills that might be beneficial when you start live trading.

Total Transparency in the Information You Get

The Forex exchange is a huge market and it operates 24 hours across different countries in various time zones. However big the market is, you get all the information you need to place trades. You will get information about the current forecast as well as the rates.

The information is real-time meaning that you get the information when it is displayed. This information is ideal for analysis so that you make deductions to the trend of the market.

Low Cost of Investment

Compared to other investments in the markets, Forex trading comes with a low cost of investment. The low cost of investment is due to the direct involvement by dealers which results in covering of risks; this means it doesn't need so much brokerage.

High Leverage

Compared to other forms of investments, Forex gives you the highest level of leverage than other investing markets. Even though you place a smaller amount of capital into the business, you have the capacity to win or lose big in the deals.

Wide Currency Pairs

When you enter the Forex market, you can trade in many currency pairs to your own advantage. With so many options to pick from, you get to enter a spot trade or opt for future agreement contracts.

You can choose the pair according to the budget or the type of risk that the pair comes with.

High Liquidity

The Forex market has the biggest number of players compared to other markets.

This leads to high liquidity that brings to the fore big players that fill large orders of the trade. It eliminates the manipulation of price, thus this promotes efficient pricing models.

High Volatility

In Forex, you can easily switch from one currency to another if you find it more profitable.

Remember that there is a high risk associated with investing capital in such a market, but with volatility, you end up with higher profit especially when you switch to a different currency that promises a good return.

This, in turn, gives you a higher advantage and increases profit.

Works for 24 Hours Each Day

The trading program operates 24 hours each day in a week which means you will always have a chance to trade no matter the situation. You can get from your day job and then handle any trades that you want during the evening.

You can take up Forex trading as a day job and you can work within the normal hours or your own preferred time. The good news is that you can still access the various tools and information that helps you to run the trades.

High Confidence Levels

When you make a profit, you get stimulated to run more trades. This creates a lot of goodwill. You can also get into the trade more thus make more money than ever.

The Disadvantages

Lack of Transparency

When you work with a brokerage, you tend to lose the transparency that needs to come automatically.

Make sure you work with a broker that follows all the rules that are involved in Forex trading.

While the market might not work under any regulations, which is a good thing, it might be constrained to the rules of the broker.

Price Determination

The platform goes through the price determination process, which is very complex. The outcome is that the rates are influenced by a host of multiple factors and reasons.

For one, the global economy and politics are a huge influence in the rate of the currency and they end up creating uncertainty in the price of the exchanges.

You have to use your technical knowledge and other indicators to determine whether you are to face a loss or not.

Many Risk Factors

There are various risk factors that are involved in Forex Trading. For instance, there is high leverage that the results in high risks.

The uncertainty comes due to the price and the currency rate which, in turn, results in high profit or loss, so you have to be focused and knowledgeable about the market.

You are Fully Responsible for the Outcome

The Forex market allows you to interact with many investors that can help you run trades successfully. However, at the end of the day, you are fully responsible for the outcomes of the trades that you place.

This is the reason many newcomers end up quitting because of the losses that they suffer when entering the market with limited knowledge of the processes.

High Volatility

We have looked at high volatility under the advantages, but depending on how you experience it, this can turn out to be a disadvantage as well.

Changes in the economy usually turn out to be an issue on the process, thus it can be difficult for you as an investor to take a risk when investing the money.

When the changes are against you, it can lead to a huge loss to the investor especially when the market goes downhill.

Market Unpredictability

The market never shuts down; this means that you, as an investor, also have to be fully attentive, so that you don't miss out on any update. You have to stay updated at all times with the trends because these get updated each minute.

The market can change at any time, and thus you have to be conscious of what is happening in the market the whole day long. This means you have to be able to sit on the computer for hours waiting for the right trend.

Overconfidence

As time goes by, the trader experiences a set of winning trades that makes them overconfident. They fail to realize that they need to take caution with every trade, ending up with losing trades.

This overconfidence makes them lose their morale because they fail to realize that trading comes with losses as well.

The Need for Education

For you to enter the Forex trading market, you need to have enough knowledge of the subject. While you can learn on the job, it is advisable that you take a course or some classes to understand what it is all about.

Many people that have entered the market without any knowledge have had to contend with losses.

Many Scammers on the Loose

Another disadvantage of this trading method is that there are too many scammers ready to grab your loot. This is why you need to identify the best broker to work with that will not cheat you and that can guarantee you better returns.

Emotional Trading

Many traders end up trading emotionally, a factor that makes them lose more than they win. The biggest emotion in trading is fear, which is due to the uncertain trading environment that you are faced with.

Chapter 4 The Position Trading Strategy

This trading technique focuses on the bigger picture of the market (weekly or monthly charts). It eliminates market noise, such as monitoring and fluctuations. You don't have to monitor the charts constantly, and you execute fewer trades. You won't overtrade and feel the temptation to enter the market daily, and it will help you survive the market volatility.

It's easier to define trends with trading divergences. The position trading strategy enables you to detect hidden divergence opportunities. Hidden divergence patterns become more obvious with higher time frames.

You are selling a currency with a low interest rate and buying a currency with a high interest rate. You are generating a profit from a difference in interest rates between the two countries.

Identify support and resistance levels. You are trading moving averages on higher time frames due to fewer false signals. It takes some time, so it is safer but without you having to spend all day in front of a computer.

One of the most important pieces of information about position trading is resistance and support. Resistance is when the price is no longer rising. Support is when the price is no longer falling. When looking into the best strategy for you to use as a position trader, you will want to ensure you understand resistance and support. It's at certain prices when you will purchase or sell a position. If you don't understand support and resistance, you won't be able to trade at the right moment.

Is Position Trading For You?

If you are more into following the bigger picture of your currency's trend, position trading is something to look into. Position traders don't focus on minor details. Instead, they look at the trends in months and years. It is the opposite of day trading, which is when you purchase your trades and sell them in one day.

If you decide you don't want to spend a lot of time trading, you will want to look into position trading. Because you focus on the long run, you don't need to worry about the day-to-day parts of trading. For example, you won't need to read the newspaper every morning or have an evening routine. Instead, your routine will focus on the times you spend checking in on your currencies.

Position trading is right for you if you're patient and not too excited about trading, and you want an investment that builds over time. Another way to know if it's your fit is how well you listen to public opinion. As a position trader, you will focus more on your thoughts and strategy than on people who tell you the country is in a recession.

As a position trader, you are going to make under four trades a year. When you look at the patterns, you will focus more on a monthly or yearly pattern. While this is investing for the long term, you don't want to limit your details too much. You want to understand what your stock is doing on at least a week-to-week basis. Furthermore, you want to analyze the trading patterns yearly. How much have they changed? Have they increased or decreased over the years? Ask yourself questions to try to understand the pattern of the currency.

How To Apply Position Trading

When it comes to position trading, you need to understand the three elements to make it a success.

1. *Planned entry.* You don't want to jump in on a currency. You want to have a plan before you go into a trade as this will give you the right mindset. You will create this plan as you are analyzing the history of the currency. You will select the point when to trade in the currency, preferably when the price is at a lower point.

2. *Planned exit.* Whenever you trade, you want to make sure that you have a strategy in place just in case something goes wrong. You always want to do what you can to eliminate loss. This includes setting a low point before you sell. This means that if the price drops below your lowest point, you sell it immediately.

3. *Controlled risk.* One of the best ways to become successful as a trader is to eliminate risk. This will go with any trading strategy you use. However, strategies will present different risks. One risk with positions trading is you don't spend enough time on investing. While you don't need to get into the day-to-day details, you do want to pay attention to price fluctuations. You also need to understand when to exit and when to have patience and wait for a low price to increase. Prices are always fluctuating in the market. Therefore, it's important not to jump to conclusions.

Another factor is you lock your capital in for a long time, such as six months to a year. Therefore, you want to ensure you will not need the money you invest in this period. This can create a risk if you don't plan. If you are putting a significant amount of money into the currency, you could find yourself needing the cash if you have an emergency. This can create a problem with loss when you sell.

Strategies to Use

1. *Breakout strategy.* When you use the breakout strategy, you will get involved in the trade during the early stages of the trend. You might make your move when the price is on the lower end, or you can choose the higher end.

2. *Range strategy.* When you use the range strategy, you will focus on purchasing investments that are oversold or overbought. Most investors use this strategy when the market is highly unpredictable and fluctuating often.

3. *Short-term strategy.* Even though position trading is known as a long-term strategy, you can use it as a short-term strategy. What this means is, instead of holding on to your investment for months or a year, you plan to

hold it for a few days or weeks. You might decide this is the best because of the trend or because you are trying out position trading. You might also use a short-term approach quickly if you made a mistake when purchasing the investment.

Pros And Cons Of Position Trading

Pros

1. Position trading is relatively easy for you to learn because it doesn't take up a lot of your time.

2. You can continue to learn about investing after you have made your first trade.

3. You can start to see a profit quickly compared to other types of trading.

4. Compared to other types of trading, your stress is lower.

5. You don't need to have a lot of capital in order to become successful.

6. You can predict the market trends easier through analysis because of this strategy's long-term nature.

Cons

1. You need to have a lot of patience.

2. You can struggle to receive regular benefits because of this strategy's long-term nature.

3. You can wait too long to make a trade, which means a higher loss. This often happens when traders want to wait for the price to increase.

4. Your money is tied up for months to a year or more.

5. If you don't understand when to trade, you can lose a lot of money. This can lead to financial hardship and depression or other psychological strains.

Tips For Beginners

If you think positions trading might be your strategy, here are a few tips to help you get started.

Think Long-Term

You need to make sure you can completely invest the money. You need to think ahead for at least a year or two. This means to take a look at where you sit financially. Ask yourself questions to make sure you can afford this investment. Do you have enough money for an emergency? Do you have any backup financial plans in case something happens?

You also want to think long-term when it comes to trends. Start by taking a look at two years ago and then a year ago before you go monthly. You don't need to care about the minute-to-minute trend unless you want to. However, it is always wise to go into daily trends. This can be something that many beginners miss because they are too focused on long-term trends. Daily trends can help you analyze charts so you know what could happen in the near future.

Set Your Entry and Exit Strategies

This is often missed with beginners because they think they can mentally keep track. The fact is, you are more likely to let your emotions take control of your decisions as a beginner. By setting your entry and exit strategies, you are able to control your emotions. You just need to make sure you follow your plan of action.

Pay Attention, but Don't Stress over Minor Fluctuations

One of the benefits of position trading is you don't have to watch your currencies on a daily basis. However, you need to be aware that this can cause you problems. One factor about the market is that it can change in a flash. This means if you go a week without checking the price fluctuations of your investment, you can find yourself with a deep loss. Therefore, you want to be cautious about price fluctuations, but you don't want to stress over them.

Always remember that just because the price reduced, it doesn't mean it will continue to. It can rise in a heartbeat; however, it can also decline. You need to understand the trends in order to help yourself through price fluctuation. You also need to keep your emotions in check.

Chapter 5 Developing Your Trading Plan

Having a strong trading plan is an important part of successfully trading on the Forex market. Even the experts develop one, so it is important that as a beginner, you do too. In this chapter, you are going to learn about why you need a roadmap and how you can develop one.

What Is a Trading Plan?

Developing a trading plan allows you to define a goal and create a system for you to work towards that goal through your trades. Due to the volatility of the market, you cannot create a finite blueprint for your trading plan. However, you can create a general strategy and goals for you to work with. There are certain rules and elements to consider when you are developing your plan to ensure that you have one that is strong and will serve you for the best.

Who Needs One?

It is important that anyone who is doing trading on the Forex market, or anywhere else for that matter, to have a strong trading plan. This allows them the opportunity to reap in all of the benefits of having a trading plan from risk management to learning discipline in your trades. Even experts develop plans before entering the Forex market, so it is imperative that as a beginner, you also develop a plan.

Why Do You Need a Trading Plan?

There are a number of benefits to having a trading plan when you are getting involved in the Forex market. For one, it is great for you to minimize your risk due to your ability to have a plan for what you will do in certain scenarios. You can also use it to establish your exit strategies beforehand so that you know when you are going to exit if necessary. Having a plan also allows you to stay focused on your goal and make large strides towards that goal, so you can stay on par for your goals with your trading decisions. Another reason why having a plan is important is because it allows you to ensure that you are constantly evaluating your trades to ensure that your money is working well for you and that you are making strong decisions. If you find that your trades aren't having high enough yields or are too risky, you can reevaluate your plan and fix your strategy for a better outcome.

General Planning Rules

There are a few plans when you are preparing to trade on the market. There are no blueprints, though there are some considerations you need to think about when you are developing the plan. The following four "rules" are important when you are in the process of creating your trading plan, to ensure that you have the best results.

- Write down your goals all the time. If you make any changes, write that down as well. You will want to write down virtually every single part of your plan. This way, you can ensure that your thoughts are organized and your plan is solid. It also helps you stay focused on your goals and work towards them with every move you make.

- Make sure that in addition to writing out your plans, you record your progress as well. This allows you to see how your plan has worked, and to learn from previous trades that you have made as well so that you can continue to learn and make better decisions. This process will give you a better opportunity to improve your trading strategies and ensure that you recall which markets you have been exposed to.

- Aside from writing everything down, you must control your finances. It is important that you manage your money properly in order to ensure that you are staying on top of everything to prevent yourself from investing too much into the market. You want to make sure that you are managing your risk and exposure and staying on top of how much you are making and losing in the grand scheme of things.

The best way to keep track of everything is to have a trading journal that allows you to keep track of your plan and all of the moves you make. It also allows you to keep track of your finances to ensure that you are making wise decisions and not investing too much or losing too much in certain moves.

Creating Your Plan

Before you create a plan, you need to ask yourself some questions. You should write these questions down in your trading journal to ensure that you are focused on what your goal is and that your plan aligns with the answers you have for the following questions.

- Why do you want to trade with Forex?

- What is your opinion on risk?

- What is the amount of time you're willing to invest in trades?

- How much do you know about trading already?

Identifying the answers to these questions is the best way to discover what your goals are with trading and how you position yourself in the market on trades that you will make. You need to answer these questions before you start creating your plan, as they are the basis for the plans that you make.

Once you answer those four primary questions, there are more you will want to consider. The answer to these will be exactly what you need to know in order to create your specific plan and move forward with it. Your answers don't need to be deep and thoughtful, but they do need to be answered clearly.

- Where are you right now, financially? Have you had any involvement in the market yet? If so, what is your involvement?

- At this time, what type of trader are you? What are your thoughts on trading and risk?

- Based on your level of knowledge right now, how confident do you feel in trading?

- What is the amount of capital you have to start your trading with?

- What are your financial goals with your trading?

- How long do you want to be trading for in order to reach that goal?

What is the success going to look like?

Answering these questions gives you a firm guideline of where you want to go and what you want to do with your trading. If you go in saying "I want to make a lot of money" but never define what "a lot" is, you are not going to be able to identify when you get there. You will also not know how to identify if you have been losing too much money. The market is something that you enter for specific purposes, as that is what will assist you in making the money you desire. You don't necessarily need to have a purpose such as retirement or education funds, but having a goal of what you want and a timeframe of when you want to achieve it will significantly assist you in mastering it and making as much as you desire.

Chapter 6 Think Before You Trade

No one can tell you exactly what the market is going to do, because it is influenced by so many different factors. Some of these factors remain a mystery even to the most experienced Forex trader. When you are starting, t is best to look at six-month support and resistance levels. These levels occur when a group of buyers and sellers find a trade that they believe is overpriced or discounted. Together, these buyers then create action in the market that changes it.

Find Supply And Resistance Levels

In order to find the supply and resistance levels look at a chart that contains six months of daily trade between two currencies that you might be interested in buying or selling. While some experts recommend that you look at a five-year period that complicates matters and makes complicates your work. Looking at periods shorter than six months, does not give you enough data to base your buying and selling decisions on.

Easy Way To Find The Level

Lay the chart on the table in front of you and get a ruler. Lay the ruler on top of the chart and move it up and down until the lines on the chart touch the ruler the most often. Draw a straight line across the paper.

Watch The Market For Dips

Now, watch the market. When the market dips below your determined level, then consider buying. Do not worry about rather the market has hit its absolute bottom or not, as you will probably make money when you buy at this point. The reason that the market dips below the line is that more people are willing to sell their shares than there are people looking to buy the share.

Watch The Market For Rises

Additionally, watch for times that the market rises above your line. These are good times to sell your stock. Again, it is not necessary to wait for the market to raise to the absolute top because no one can tell you exactly when that will occur and you do not want to miss the opportunity. The reason that the market rises above the line is that there are more people wanting to buy the share than there are people looking to sell the share.

Eliminate Confusion

While many experts will try to confuse you by having you look at multiple trading strategies including moving average convergence-divergence (MACD), stochastics, and relative strength indicators, your charts will become so messy that it will be difficult to spot the trends. It will also become difficult for the brain that is trying to assimilate all the new information to make sense of the information.

Master The Basics

Once you master the basics of supply and resistance levels, then you can begin adding more complex trading strategies if you desire. Be forewarned, however, that these additional trading strategies often result in making less money.

Chapter 7 Trading Strategies

Forex Scalping Strategies

Making fast money with Forex is what we all desire. There are various scalping strategies in Forex however, most of those strategies may be difficult to follow or may just not work. Though, the fastest method of making money in trading is through scalping.

Scalping can be defined as a fast-paced style of trading which specializes in making fast profits on small price changes, often times, after entering a trade that became profitable. It is one of the most important trading strategies in Forex. It requires the trader to stick to a precise exit strategy and is often done on the lower time frames including M1, M2, and M15.

Traders get trading opportunities by searching for small price changes within the market. In scalping, it is important to have prompt execution as well as precise timing. Although this method of trading has some risks, it still yields some profit to some traders. Because of the need to capitalize quickly on opportunities that become available, a scalp trader is likened to a marathon runner.

You must always remember that a huge loss can nullify whatever little gains the trader has obtained through Forex scalping. Due to the fact that most scalpers are not patient enough to wait for other opportunities to become available for a trade, the profitable trade becomes a loss as the opportunities reduce. To an extent, scalping exploits leveraging which makes people stay away from it. Being too greedy or trading too big is not advisable in scalping as these are easy methods of losing lots of money.

Having the focus to place trades, the proper tools, as well as a low spread broker is necessary for the success of this strategy. The following are factors which help scalpers make decisions:

- Your daily trades should be based on the watch list of hot stocks you create.

- Buy breakouts and watch observe an immediate up move after entry.

- In the absence of a move up, sell immediately.

- To ensure high percentage accuracy, once you have a little profit, sell half and adjust exit to your entry point on the position remaining.

- Take 3 – 5 trades until you have achieved your daily target.

Liquidity is a vital part of scalping as traders get in and out of their trades at different times in a day. Additionally, it guarantees that the best prices are gotten by trades as they get in and out of trades.

To make a profit, scalpers keep up with the latest news and future events which will likely cause price movements. They also tend to observe the low and high prices of a currency pair during a trading session and estimate the direction over a short term. This, however, requires high concentration and immediate execution.

Setting profit target amount per trade is another means of making a profit, and it ought to be relative to how much the currency pair is. Scalpers are expected to have a win/loss ratio of more than 50% so as to make a profit.

Different Timeframes

Try to consider the timeframe before you begin trading. This could be as low as the 1M chart in which the candle is formed every minute, to monthly charts formed once in a month. Do not forget that unless you are trading with the range bars that are totally immune to the time factor, all candles last for a particular time period.

In terms of trading, whatever is less than the hourly time frame should be seen as a short term. Examples of short-term trading include scalp swings and scalping. Hourly timeframes and other time frames less than a daily timeframe are classified as medium-term and are best considered for intraday and intra-week swing trading.

Time frames considered as long-term are daily, weekly, and monthly charts. In these timeframes, trades are usually executed 4-5 times in a year and do not just happen regularly. Do not forget that if you lose focus and are distracted from your charts, a 1M chart trading strategy has a really high probability of overwhelming you.

Scalping Indicators In Forex

Due to the fact that there are many poor indicators, getting a good indicator could be difficult, here are some that can be used.

- Forex Scalping of Multiple Charts Strategy

- Ribbon Entry Forex Trading Strategy

- The Relative Strength and Weakness Exit Strategy

These strategies although may seem like those used on longer time frames, they can actually be modified for trading on small-time frames like a 2 minute or 5-minute chart. A range bound market with little interference from fundamental factors is usually the best when implementing any scalping strategy. Poor performance in scalping arises during times of trend movement as well as volatility.

Forex Scalping of Multiple Charts: One of the best to implement in forex scalping as well as one of my favorites is this strategy. A 15- minute time frame of your preferred chart should be pulled up in order to set this up. Ensure that there are no indicators on the chart and then set up 3 horizontal lines which you then use for a 45-90-minute trading session. The first line indicates the opening print while the remaining two are to show the low and high trading range.

There is a need to also set up this on a 2- minute time frame after monitoring the price action at the three levels. When the resistance and the scalp support line up on both timeframes, you'll get the highest profits.

Ribbon Entry Forex Strategy: Placing the simple moving average (SMA) 5-8-13 combination on a 2 minutes chart, is the major objective of this scalping strategy. This helps to ascertain what trades are to be sold or bought on counter swings in the small trends. It is easy to master this strategy or method as it only needs the 5-8-13 ribbon to be lined up. Where it will then, point to either lower or higher during solid trends. A diminished momentum is determined by penetration in the 13 bar SMA which then favors a reversal.

The ribbon will become flat at the swings and range-bound periods and the price may also pass the ribbon sometimes. The changeover would then be observed by the scalper when the ribbon turns both lower and higher.

The Relative Strength and Weakness Exit Strategy: This simple method of scalping is about finding out when the best time to cut losses and take profits in short term scalping trades is. This is of great importance. Using the 5-3-3 stochastic indicator as well as ribbon signals and an SD Bollinger band works well on markets like the indices.

The best method of ribbon trades works when stochastic turn to become lower than the overbought level, or higher than the oversold level. Ensure your exit is timed correctly; observe the interaction with the band at a particular price. The concrete bands predict the trend, making it the best point to take profit. Retracement in the market is something Forex scalping strategies cannot afford to undergo.

As the stochastic indicator rolls over giving you a signal to leave the trade, ensure you take time to exit the trade. This exit signal could be the inability of the price to penetrate the band.

A Simple Scalping Setup

Lagging and signal delays can make Forex scalping extremely difficult. This sometimes makes it more profitable to use a price action scalping system without indicators. You will know what to do from the price. Your best indicator and signal are the price. As long as you adhere to the risk management recommendations and rules, you should be able to get good profits using the following scalping system.

Even if you have not traded with Forex in the past, this scalping strategy is very easy to use for every trader and does not make use of difficult rules. This system does not make it necessary for a trader to follow essential Forex rules such; as ignore signals against a trend, do not trade against a trend, as the system itself confirms trend following.

Scalping is difficult for amateurs; ensure you practice with the system on your demo account for a month's trial before going live.

This could be the best Forex scalping strategy for new traders, and it is a trend following strategy. It also has the added advantage of being easy to apply on the 1-, 5-, and 15-minute chart trading.

Currency Pairs: USD/JPY, USD/CHF EUR/USD, AUD/USD, NZD/USD and GBP/USD

Time Frame: 1m to 15m

Indicators:

Stochastic (STO) (14, 3, 3) with levels 10 and 90

Bollinger bands (BB) (14 period) (green)

Buy position: The price first needs to broke down below the lower Bollinger Band. Now, wait till the candle closes in the Bollinger Band again. Stochastic should be crossing up 10 from below 10.

Sell position: The price first needs to be broken above the upper Bollinger Band. Then wait until the candle closes in the Bollinger Band again. The stochastic should be crossing down 90 from above 90.

Forex Risks To Be Wary Of

Most foreign exchange trades are made up of foreign exchange swaps, spot transactions, currency swaps, futures, and options. Because it is a leveraged product, the risks associated with forex trades are much and can lead to significant losses.

Losses related to forex trading might be larger than that expected at first as a result of all the risks associated with it. A small initial payment can lead to illiquid assets and a significant amount of losses, because of how leveraged trades are designed. Also, political issues, as well as time differences, could lead to serious consequences on countries' currencies and financial markets. Although the trading volume in the forex market is the highest, there are obvious risks which could cause significant losses.

Interest Rate Risks: Basic macroeconomics courses teach that interest rates affect a country's exchange rates. Increase in a country's interest rates will lead to a stronger currency because of the influx of investments in the country's assets, as it is believed that a stronger currency leads to higher returns. Contrarily, as the interest rates reduce, the currency becomes weak because investors start to take back their investments. The differences between currency values can lead to drastic changes in forex prices because of the nature of the interest rate and its indirect effect on exchange rates.

Leverage Risks: In order to gain access to significant trades in foreign currencies, a margin, which is a small initial investment, required by leverage in forex trading is needed. Small price fluctuations lead to margin call where the investor is expected to pay an additional margin. Aggressive use of leverage would lead to significant loss of investments and investors when the market conditions are volatile. The interest differences between currencies can lead to a dramatic change in forex prices.

Transaction Risks; These are risks associated with transactions. Transaction risks are referred to as the unstable exchange rate from the initial time a contract was made to the time it is finalized. In Forex trading, when contracts are made, it is very possible for the exchange rate to change before the contract is concluded. The trading hour for Forex is 24 hours. During this time, the same currency can be sold or bought at varying prices at different times. The higher the time interval between the beginning of a contract and its conclusion, the greater the transaction risks. Whenever there is a change in the exchange rate due to this time difference, the cost of the transaction becomes very high.

The Counterparty Risk; A counterparty risk is a risk of defaults caused by the supplier in any business. A counterparty refers to the brokers or suppliers of assets to investors. They are the companies that provide the services or valuables to others known as investors. In Forex, there are contracts known as spot contracts and forward contracts. Spot contracts deal with spot currencies, and in this trade, the risk may result from the brokers or market makers. There might be a breach of contract by the counterparty if the market conditions are not favorable.

Country Risk; When considering your options before making investments especially in currencies, make sure you consider the solidity and standard of the country issuing it. Exchange rates of developing countries or underdeveloped countries around the world depend on the currencies of other great countries like the United State dollar. Therefore, central banks must exercise efficient measures to maintain fixed exchange rates. Once the currency is devalued, it can affect Forex trade. Currency devaluation is as a result of recurring balance of a payment deficit, a condition where the rate at which a country imports goods and services is higher than the rate it exports.

Investments are not based on facts and investigation, but rather based on supposition. Therefore, once an investor feels the value of a currency will soon reduce, he removes his assets. This act, however, causes the value of the currency to reduce more. The investors that will still be trading the currency, will discover that their assets are not easily sold or exchanged. In Forex, currency crisis leads to assets not being sold, credit risk and further devaluation of the currency.

Chapter 8 Fundamental Analysis

In order to trade in the forex market successfully, one of the most important things you can learn is the most reliable way to spot a trade that is going to end up being reliably profitable from one that blows up in your face. This is where proper analysis comes in handy, whether technical or fundamental. Fundamental analysis is easier to learn, though it is more time consuming to use properly, while technical analysis can be more difficult to wrap your mind around but can be done quite quickly once you get the hang of it. While both will help you to find the information you are looking for, they go about doing so in different ways; fundamental analysis concerns itself with looking at the big picture while technical analysis focuses on the price of a given currency in the moment to the exclusion of all else.

This divide when it comes to information means that fundamental analysis will always be useful when it coms to determining currencies that are currently undervalued based on current market forces. The information that is crucial to fundamental analysis is generated by external sources which means there won't always be new information available at all times. This chapter and the next are dedicated to fundamental and technical analysis, respectively.

Generally speaking, fundamental analysis allows you a likely glimpse at the future of the currency in question based on a variety of different variables such as publicized changes to the monetary policy that the countries you are interested in might affect. The idea here is that with enough information you can then find currency pairs that are currently undervalued because the market hasn't yet had the time to catch up with the changes that have been made. Fundamental analysis is always made up of the same set of steps which are described in detail below.

Start by determining the baseline: When it comes to considering the fundamental aspects of a pair of currencies, the first thing that you are going to want to do is to determine a baseline from which those currencies tend to return to time and again compared to the other commonly traded currency pairs. This will allow you to determine when it is time to make a move as you will be able to easily pinpoint changes to the pair that are important enough to warrant further consideration.

In order to accurately determine the baseline, the first thing you will need to do is to look into any relevant macroeconomic policies that are currently affecting your currency of choice. You will also want to look into the available historical data as past behavior is one of the best indicators of future evets. While this part of the process can certainly prove tedious, their important cannot be overstated.

After you have determined the historical precedent of the currency pair you are curious about, the next thing you will want to consider is the phase the currency is currently in and how likely it is going to remain in that phase for the foreseeable future. Every currency goes through phases on a regular basis as part of the natural market cycle.

The first phase is known as the boom phase which can be easily identified by its low volatility and high liquidity. The opposite of this phase is known as the bust phase wherein volatility is extremely high, and liquidity is extremely low. There are also pre and post versions of both phases that can be used to determine how much time the phase in question has before it is on its way out. Determining the right phase is a key part of knowing when you are on the right track regarding a particular trading pair.

In order to determine the current major or minor phase, the easiest thing to do is to start by checking the current rates of defaults along with banks loans as well as the accumulated reserve levels of the currencies in question. If numbers are relatively low them a boom phase is likely to be on its way, if not already in full swing. If the current numbers have already overstayed their welcome, then you can be fairly confident that a post-boom phase is likely to start at any time. Alternatively, if the numbers in question are higher than the baseline you have already established then you know that the currency in question is either due for a bust phase or is already experiencing it.

You can make money from either of the major phases as long as you are aware of them early on enough to turn a profit before things start to swing back in the opposite direction. Generally speaking, this means that the faster you can pinpoint what the next phase is going to be, the greater your dividends of any related trades will be.

Broaden your scope: After you have a general idea of the baseline for your favored currencies, as well as their current phases, the next thing you will need to do is look at the state of the global market as a whole to determine how it could possibly affect your trading pair. To ensure this part of the process is as effective as possible you are going to need to look beyond the obvious signs that everyone can see to find the indicators that you know will surely make waves as soon as they make it into the public consciousness.

One of the best places to start looking for this information is in the technology sector as emerging technologies can turn entire economies around in a relatively short period of time.

Technological indicators are often a great way to take advantage of a boom phase by getting in on the ground floor as, once it starts, it is likely to continue for as long as it takes for the technology to be fully integrated into the mainstream. Once it reaches the point of complete saturation then a bust phase is likely going to be on the horizon, and sooner rather than later. If you feel as though the countries responsible for the currencies in question are soon going to be in a post-boom or post-bust phase, then you are going to want to be very careful in any speculative market as the drop-off is sure to be coming and it is difficult to pinpoint exactly when.

If you know that a phase shift is coming, but you aren't quite sure when, then it is a good idea to focus on smaller leverage amounts than during other phases as they are more likely to pay off in the short-term. At the same time, you are also going to want to keep any eye out for long-term positions that are likely to pay out if a phase shift does occur. On the other hand, if the phase you are in currently is just starting out, you can make trades that have a higher potential for risk as the time concerns aren't going to be nearly serious enough to warrant the additional caution.

Look to global currency policy: While regional concerns are often going to be able to provide you with an insight into some long-reaching changes a given currency might experience in the near future, you are also going to want to broaden your search, even more, to include relevant global policies as well. While determining where you are going to start can be difficult at first, all you really need to do is to provide the same level of analysis that you used at the micro level on a macro basis instead. The best place to start with this sort of thing is going to be with the interest rates of the major players including the Federal Reserve, the European Central Bank, the Bank of Japan, the Bank of England and any other banks that may affect the currencies you are considering trading.

You will also need to consider any relevant legal mandates or policy biases that are currently in play to make sure that you aren't blindsided by these sorts of things when the times actually comes to stop doing research and actually make a move. While certainly time consuming, understanding every side of all the major issues will make it far easier to determine if certain currencies are flush with supply where the next emerging markets are likely to appear and what worldwide expectations are when it comes to future interest rate changes as well as market volatility.

Don't forget the past: Those who forget the past are doomed to repeat it and that goes double for forex traders. Once you have a solid grasp on the current events of the day, you are going to want to dig deeper and look for scenarios in the past that match what is currently going on today. This level of understanding will ultimately lead to a greater understanding of the current strength of your respective currencies while also giving you an opportunity to accurately determine the length of the current phase as well.

In order to ensure you are able to capitalize on your knowledge as effectively as possible, the ideal time to jump onto a new trade is going to be when one of the currency pairs is entering a post-boom phase while the other is entering the post-bust phase. This will ensure that the traditional credit channels are not exhausted completely, and you will thus have access to the maximum amount of allowable risk of any market state. This level of risk is going to start dropping as soon as the market conditions hit an ideal state and will continue until the situation with the currencies is reversed so getting in and making a profit when the time is right is crucial to your long-term success.

Don't forget volatility: Keeping the current level of volatility in mind is crucial when it comes to ensuring that the investments you are making are actually going to pay off in a reasonable period of time. Luckily, Luckily, it is relatively easy to determine the current level of volatility in a given market, all you need to do is to look to that country's stock market. The greater the level of stability the market in question is experiencing, the more confident those who are investing in it are going to remain when means the more stable the forex market is going to remain as well.

Additionally, it is important to keep in mind that, no matter what the current level of volatility may be, the market is never truly stable. As such, the best traders are those who prepare for the worst while at the same time hoping for the best. Generally speaking, the more robust a boom phase is, the lower the overall level of volatility is going to be.

Think outside the box on currency pairs: All of the information that you gather throughout the process should give you a decent idea regarding the current state of the currency pairs you are keeping tabs on. You should now have enough to be able to use this information to determine which pairs are going to be able to provide you with the most potential profit in not just the short-term but the long-term as well. Specifically, you are going to want to keep an eye out for pairs that have complimentary futures so that they will end up with the greatest gap between their two interest rates as possible.

Additionally, you are going to want to consider the gap between countries when it comes to overall output and unemployment rate. When looking into these differences you are also going to need to be aware of the fact that shortages can cause constraints to capacity or when the unemployment rate drops, both of which can lead to inflation as well. This, in turn, leads to an increase in interest rates which leads to a general cooling of the country's economy. As such, these factors are extremely important when it comes to determining the overall disparity between the interest rates of specific countries in the near future.

Furthermore, you are going to want to keep tabs on the amount of debt that the countries in question are dealing with, as well as their reputation of repayment on the global market. Specifically, you are going to want to look for a balanced capital to debt ratio as the healthier that this number is the stronger the national currency is going to be no matter what else is currently taking place. To determine this ratio, you will want to know how much capital each country currently has on hand as well as their position when it comes to other nations and their level of reserves and foreign investment.

Understand their relative trade strength: If you find a currency that is currently in the middle of a boom phase, the overall strength that its fundamentals show will determine how likely those who are holding it in various currency pairs are to hold or sell. The same also goes for currencies that boast an overly strong or overly weak interest rate when compared to other, similar currencies. What this means is that when a given currency is in the earliest part of the boom phase you will be able to easily find a strong market for its related currency pairs which combine agreeable fundamentals and strong interest rates. While all of these factors are important, as a general rule a strong interest rate will always trump subpar fundamentals.

Watch out for market sentiment

While determining specifics in undervalued currencies is useful most of the time, sometimes the market simply doesn't behave in the way that it realistically should. In these cases, it is the market sentiment that has hijacked the price of the currency in question and learning how to stay on the lookout for its influence is guaranteed to save you from some seriously unprofitable trades in the long run.

Like many things in the forex market, this is easier said than done, however, which is why it is best to take the following suggestions related to reading market sentiment to heart if you ever hope to get a clear idea of how strong the momentum regarding a given currency truly is.

Choose the right trend: Each and every move that a currency makes is ultimately based on a trend that started building hours, if not days before. As such, if you spend time trading with either the 15 or 60-minute chart then you may find yourself accidentally moving forward based on part of a larger trend that is ultimately going to end up moving in the opposite direction. As such, in order to avoid such mistakes, you are going to want to start by identifying the trend in the daily chart and then working inward from there until you reach your target chart. This will allow you to more easily determine the breadth of a given chart and allow you to avoid trading based on anterior movement as well.

Find the right price movement: On the topic of price movement, depending on the pair you are trading in, you will likely come across profits that you might not otherwise bank by simply getting a feel for the way your favored currency pairs move on a regular basis. Getting a feel for price movement means understanding the speed at which the pair typically moves, in both directions, to ensure that you know the most effective time to strike.

When the movement is clearly headed in an upwards direction with a quickness, only to slowly descend after the fact, time and again, then you can expect other traders to be steadily buying into the pair without taking the time to do all the relevant research. This, in turn, means you can expect the overall sentiment of the market to be bullish which means you can respond appropriately.

Similar information can also be determined based on the way the market responds when new relevant information, both positive and negative, comes to light. As an example, if there was just a round of positive economic news out of the United Kingdom but the positive change in the GBP and USD pair doesn't seem all that enthusiastic, then you can safely determine that the market is moving in a bearish direction when it comes to GBP/USD.

Watch your indicators of volume: While there are a wide variety of different indicators that measure volume, there are no better means for doing so than the Commitment of Traders Report which is released each and every Friday. This report clearly outlines the net of all the trades made, both long and short, for the week, for both commercial and private traders. This is a great place to start if you aren't sure what currencies to favor as this will show where most of the interest was for the proceeding week.

As previously noted, it is best to always trade on the trend which means that if there are more net longs overall you are going to want to buy and if there are more net shorts overall then you are going to want to sell. When this is not the case is if the buy positions are already at extreme levels then you will want to sell or at least wait until things move in the other direction because there can be no more increase if everyone who is going to buy has already bought. Eventually, you will see a reversal in this case which means that if this is the case then you are better off trading in the medium term instead.

Look more closely at international trends: When you are first getting your start in the forex market you are likely going to be surprised at just how interconnected the world as a whole really is. While some of these connections are going to be obvious, other will certainly catch you off guard the first time you encounter them which means you will want to pay attention to the way news affects various currency pairs, even if you are not actually trading in them at the moment as you never know when that information might be useful again at a later date.

Chapter 9 Trading Journals

This chapter will teach you how to create a trading journal. Read this material carefully: trading journals can help you become a successful forex trader.

The Importance of Trading Journals

According to experienced traders, discipline is more important than accuracy. It would be almost impossible to determine all the crucial indicators every time. But with self-discipline, you'll know the "when", "what", and "how" of your trading strategies easily.

Recording your thoughts and transactions in a journal is one of the best ways to develop self-discipline. In fact, most people in the investing world keep a journal of some sort. They use the journal to record their initial capital, entry points, and intended exit points. Often, they also list down the rationale of their investing/trading decisions. That means they can review their previous choices and make the necessary adjustments.

Important Note: Trading journals can help you learn from your mistakes and avoid unnecessary risks.

Setting Up Your Trading Journal

Creating a trading journal consists of three steps:

First Step: Generating a Currency Checklist

Your journal should begin with a printable spreadsheet. You'll fill out and print this spreadsheet on a daily basis. The checklist will help you in "understanding" the market and identifying potential trades.

Make sure that your checklist has all of the available currency pairs. Save these pairs in the leftmost column of the spreadsheet. Then, label the next three columns as "Current", "Low", and "High", respectively. Add the indicators on the right side of the file. If you want to keep things simple, you may focus on the four primary currency pairs, namely: GBP/USD, USD/CHF, EUR/USD, and USD/JPY. You may add more currencies once you gain more trading experience.

The checklist might appear to be complex and lengthy, but you should be able to fill it out in just twenty minutes. Remember that the goal of the checklist is to present the trends and trading ranges present in the currency market. Acquiring these pieces of information is a huge step towards huge profits from forex. Without a detailed idea about the market, you will blindly trade currencies.

You will pick assets based on breakouts and prevailing trends. Unfortunately, this undisciplined approach often leads to huge losses.

Important Note: Market trends can give you excellent profit potential. If a pair is on an uptrend, you should buy it during retracements. If the trend is downward, however, you should sell during a rally.

The initial column of your spreadsheet's indicator group must be labeled as "ADX (14) > 25". ADX (i.e. Average Directional Index) is one of the most popular tools for evaluating trends. A trend exists if the value of the index is higher than 25. In general, high index values indicate strong trends.

The second column relies on "Bollinger bands". Strong trends usually hit one of the said bands. The third, fourth, and fifth columns, on the other hand, will hold the long-term SMAs (i.e. simple moving averages). If the numbers go below or above the averages, the market might be on a trend. You can verify the trend by checking crossovers (if any) that are in the trend's direction.

The group's first column will contain the Average Directional Index. This time, however, you'll look for an ADX that is lower than 25. These index values indicate weak trends. The remaining columns will contain the RSI (i.e. Relative Strength Index), traditional oscillators, and stochastic. You should conduct range trading when you have a weak ADX, high technical resistance, and oversold/overbought levels of stochastic and RSI.

Important Note: The resulting sheet can be of great help in your forex transactions. However, they are not guaranteed to work all the time. The goal of this spreadsheet is to open your eyes to the current status of the currency market.

Second Step: Identifying Potential Trades

The next part of your journal displays the trades you can make for the current trading day. Use the spreadsheet you created earlier to complete this part. Here is a basic example:

December 18, 2016

Buy USD/JPY - .8999 break (high of the previous day)

Stop at 8800 (30-day SMA).

First Target - 0.9000 (based on Fibonacci retracement)

Second Target - 0.9200 (upper Bollinger)

Third Target - Lowest point of the past ten trading days

This approach gives you clear courses of action once your desired entry price level appears. You will know the best action to take, as well as the ideal spots for your limits and stops. Keep yourself updated regarding the market conditions while working on this part of your journal.

Third Step: Listing Down the Current and/or Completed Trades

This part helps you in enforcing self-discipline. It also aids in turning your mistakes into learning opportunities. Whenever a trading day ends, take the time to review the results of your transactions. Why did you profit from a deal? What made you choose the wrong currency pair?

The main goal of this part is to determine trends and mistakes. It is likely that you are making mistakes. However, you won't know which of your actions and/or plans are faulty if you won't analyze them in detail. That means recording your transactions can help you understand your thoughts and behaviors as a forex trader. The entries in this part should look like this:

December 5, 2016

Transaction: Short 5 lots of GBP/USD @ 1.2000

Stop: 1.2500 (current all-time high)

Current Target: 1.1500

Result: The transaction got completed on the next trading day. I exited the position @ 1.300.

Comments: I thought the price will drop soon, so I didn't exit at my predetermined stopping point.

Lesson: Stick to your trading plan.

According to forex experts, an excellent trade is a trade whose fundamental and technical results match. Consequently, you shouldn't submit orders based on technical or fundamental analysis alone.

Choosing the Market Indicators

After setting up your journal, you should choose the market indicators to include in your analysis. Many forex traders fail because they consider their preferred indicators as foolproof. For example, some traders perform trades based solely on the levels of stochastic. But this strategy can result to huge losses when the currency market starts to trend. You should learn how to adapt to the changes in the market if you want to survive in the world of forex.

As a trader, you should always consider the environmental factors of the market. Prepare a list of factors so you can easily determine whether the market is range-bound or trending. Expert forex traders will tell you that selecting trade parameters plays an important role in forex.

The selection of parameters is important in every market. However, it is of the most importance in the forex market. That's because about 80% of all forex transactions are speculative. It is not surprising for currencies to stay in a specific trading environment over the long-term. In addition, the forex market is compatible with technical analysis (mainly because of the former's size).

Forex experts divide market environments into two types: trending and range trading. And defining the current market environment is the initial step of an effective trade.

Important Note: In Forex-related analyses, the shortest period of time that you can use is 24 hours. Use this timeframe even if you are making five-minute transactions.

Step 1: Profiling the Environment

Forex traders use various methods in determining the trading environment. There are many people who use visuals. But it would be best if you'll set specific rules in guiding your transactions. Here are some of the most popular rules today:

- Ranges

- ADX < 20 - The ADX is an excellent indicator of a trend's strength. Indices that are lower than 20 suggest weak trends. As you probably know, weak trends often occur in range-bound markets. If the ADX is on a downtrend, the environment will likely stay in its current condition for some time.

- Decreasing Volatility - There is a wide range of techniques that you can use in analyzing volatility. The simplest approach, however, involves comparing the short-term and long-term volatility of the market. If the short-term volatility falls after surpassing the highest point of the long-term volatility, the range trading situation is likely to reverse.

- Volatility heightens if one or more currency pairs experience fast movements. It lowers when the trading activities are quiet and the ranges aren't wide. You can use Bollinger bands to track the volatility of the market. Narrow bands indicate small ranges and low volatility. Wide bands, on the other hand, reflect wide ranges and highly volatile trading environments.

- Risk Reversals - Risk reversals consist of two options (i.e. a "put" option and a "call" option) on a currency. Their sensitivity and expiration are the same as that of the spot rate. Theoretically speaking, the volatility of the put and call options must be similar. But these options show different levels of volatility in the real world.

- You can obtain crucial data through risk reversals. In fact, many traders use these reversals to evaluate existing positions.

- Trends

-       ADX > 20 - During a trending market, you should search for a rising ADX that is higher than 25. If the AFX is higher than 25 but is downward sloping, it might be a sign that the trend will disappear soon.

-       Momentum and Trend Direction - Aside from using ADX, you should also check the market's momentum indicators. Your goal is to find a momentum that matches the trend's overall direction. During an uptrend, for instance, traders will search for upward RSI, moving averages, MACD (i.e. moving average convergence/divergence), and stochastic.

During a down trend, traders will want the said indicators to start a downward trend. If your moving averages show a perfect alignment, the momentum has considerable strength. Here are some examples of perfect alignment:

- During an uptrend - 10-day moving average > 20-day moving average > 50-day moving average, with the 100- and 200-day moving average under the short-term moving averages.

- During a downtrend - The long-term moving averages are above the short-term moving averages.

- Options - When the market is trending, you should look for reversals that favor puts or calls.

Step 2 - Identify the Time Horizon

Profiling the trading environment is not enough; you should also specify the timeframe of your intended trade. Here are some indicators and guidelines that traders use. Note that your trades don't have to meet all of the guidelines below. However, excellent trades tend to meet most of these guidelines.

- Range Trading - Intraday

- The Rules

- *Identify entry points using hourly charts.*

- *Confirm the existence of range trades through daily charts.*

- *To find entry points within a range, you may use oscillators.*

- *Search for RSIs or stochastic that reach extreme levels. These indicate reversals in the oscillators.*

- *Trades are strong when currency values maintain support levels. You have to use moving averages and the Fibonacci retracement technique for this.*

- The Indicators

  - o RSI

  - o MACD

- o Options

- o Stochastic

- o Bollinger bands

- o Fibonacci retracement

- Range Trading - Medium-Term

- The Rules

- *Focus on daily charts.*

- *You have two choices:*

  - o Look for upcoming opportunities - Search for volatile markets, where long-term volatility levels are considerably lower than short-term ones.

  - o Play in current ranges - Identify active ranges using Bollinger bands.

- *Search for one or more reversals in the market oscillators (e.g. stochastic).*

- *Check the price action - the price should fall at important resistance points and rise on important support points. You can use the traditional indicators for this task.*

- *Make sure that the ADX is lower than 25. A falling ADX is great, but not mandatory.*

- The Indicators

- *RSI*

- *MACD*

- *Options*

- *Stochastic*

- *Bollinger bands*

- *Fibonacci retracement*

- Trend Trading - Medium-Term

- The Rules

- *Find trends using daily charts. Check weekly charts to prove the existence of trends.*

- *Analyze the market's characteristics. What parameters are satisfied?*

- *Go for retracement/breakout situations on moving averages or Fibonacci levels.*

- *The trade shouldn't have any significant resistance levels in front of it.*

- *Check your trade using candlestick patterns.*

- *Enter the market during significant lows or highs.*

- *It would be best if you'll wait for the contraction of volatilities before entering the market.*

- *The fundamental characteristics of the currency pairs (e.g. growth) should be positive.*

- The Indicators
- *RSI*

- *Elliott waves*

- *Fibonacci retracement*

- *ADX*

- *Parabolic SAR (i.e. Stop and Reversal)*

- *Ichimoku Clouds*

- Breakout Trading - Medium-Term

- The Rules

- *Concentrate on daily charts.*

- *Search for contractions in the short-term volatility levels. The contraction point should be way much lower than the long-term volatility levels.*

- *Confirm breaks using pivot points.*

- *The moving averages should favor the trade.*

- The Indicators

- *Fibonacci Levels*

- *Moving Averages*

- *Bollinger Bands*

Managing Risks

The concept of risk management is easy to understand. However, many traders fail to consider it when choosing, buying, holding, and selling currencies. There are countless situations where profitable positions became losing ones, and excellent strategies became horrible financial blunders. Your IQ and your knowledge about the market don't guarantee success in the forex market. If you pay little attention to risk management, your trades will likely lead to losses.

In a nutshell, risk management consists of defining the risks you can shoulder and the profits you want to get. Without these pieces of information, chances are you will exit the market prematurely or remain in losing market positions. It is not uncommon for forex traders to have more profitable positions than losing ones, but end up with huge losses instead of profits.

The following guidelines will help you in managing risks:

- Stop-Loss Orders - These orders assist you in specifying maximum losses. By setting a stop-loss order, you can prevent horrible positions from ruining the profitability of your entire portfolio. A trailing stop is particularly useful in securing your earnings. Successful traders usually adjust their stops whenever their assets increase in value. Meanwhile, some traders close a segment of their existing positions.

- Treat new transactions as if they are independent ones, regardless of whether your positions are winning or not. This approach is excellent if you want to ride a trend or gain more profitable positions. When adding to an existing position, analyze the currency as if it is not in your portfolio yet. If the favorable trend continues, you may close a segment of your position while adjusting your stops. This task requires you to consider the rewards you want to get and the risks you can shoulder.

- How to Use Stop-Loss Orders - Because money management is important in successful forex trading, you should always implement stop-loss orders in your positions. Keep in mind that these orders specify the highest amount of loss that you'll experience. If the value of the currency hits your stopping point, your position will close quickly and automatically. Thus, utilizing stop-loss orders can greatly reduce the risks involved in your trades.

- Placing a Stop-Loss Order on Your Trades - Traders implement stop-loss orders in two ways:

- Parabolic SAR - You'll find this indicator in most forex charting computer programs. In a nutshell, Parabolic SAR shows the best position for the stop-loss order as a dot.

- Two-Day Low Approach - With this approach, you will place the order 10 pips lower than the pair's two-day low. For instance, if the pair's current value is 1.1300 and its two-day low was 1.1280, you should place the stop at 1.1270.

- Risk-Reward Ratios - You must specify the risk-reward ratio of all your trades. Basically, this ratio states that amount you can lose, and the amount you want to earn. Your ratios should be 1:2 or better. Setting these ratios before entering the market can help you avoid financial losses.

The Psychological Aspects of Currency Trading

Choosing the right indicators and monitoring the trading environment can certainly help you in your trading adventures. However, you cannot underestimate the effects of your psychological outlook on your trades. By having the appropriate psychological outlook, you can boost your chances of succeeding in the forex market.

Controlling Your Emotions

Do not allow your emotions to affect your trading decisions. The most successful traders display emotional detachment: they don't build emotional connections with the assets they acquire. They consider objectivity as an important part of their toolbox. Unskilled traders, on the other hand, make huge mistakes because they base their trades on their emotions. They switch to another plan after experiencing some losses, or become reckless after getting some profits.

Taking a Break

If you are experiencing consecutive losses, you should avoid trading to stop greed and/or fear from influencing your decisions.

You will face unprofitable transactions over the course of your trading career. Thus, you should be prepared to cope with financial losses. Traders, even the best ones, experience losing streaks. To succeed, however, you should display tenacity and concentration while going through such rough times.

Stop trading when you are on a losing streak. In most cases, forgetting about the market for several days is an effective solution to your dilemma. Sticking to your trading routine in an unfavorable market condition can lead to huge losses. And these losses can destroy your self-confidence and psychological condition. Accept your mistakes. It would be impossible to profit from all of your transactions. You will make mistakes; and your ultimate goal is to keep the damaging effects of your errors at a manageable level.

Here are some rules that you should remember:

- Do not go against the trend.

- Determine the expectations in the market.

- Define the risk-reward ratio of your trades.

- Allow your returns to increase.

- Minimize your losses.

- Secure sufficient capital.

- If you have a losing position, don't add to it.

- Record your thoughts and actions using a journal.

- Assign maximum losses or profit retracements.

- Make sure that your positions have logical sizes.

Chapter 10 Engulfing Pattern Trading With 3ms Principles

Engulfing pattern is one of my favorite trading setups. Identifying good engulfing bars can help you yield big potential profits. Yet, there are also a lot of false signals in the market. Let's refer to the below example.

As can be seen, the market had formed a strong resistance level at 1.5091 (the red horizontal line) before the engulfing pattern appeared (see the first two arrows). The market failed to break the resistance level twice, which clearly indicates how strong the resistance is. You can see the resistance remains unbreakable two more times (the third and fourth arrow) before becoming a very strong support later (notice the fifth arrow).

The engulfing pattern in the picture did NOT appear on a resistance level, meaning that its chances to attract seller pressure is not so high. Hence, it failed to work as a reversal signal. In these cases, it is advisable not to enter any trades. You are not stacking the odds in your favor when the candlesticks have not reached key support and resistance level.

Principle 1: Do not trade any candlestick pattern if it is not present on a key support or resistance level.

Let's take a look at another example when an engulfing pattern that does not meet all entry criteria may bring unexpected losses to traders.

In this case, a daily engulfing pattern was present at a strong resistance area, which meets the first condition of a turnaround. However, it failed to start a reversal of the trend. We are going to look at a smaller time frame to see the reason behind its failure to initiating a downtrend.

In the 4-hour chart, things are much clearer. First, please be noted that the engulfing pattern on the daily time frame is the totally highlighted area in yellow in the picture.

From the 4-hour chart, it is obvious that the market was creating a strong upward trend from A to H. Afterwards, the H1 low was formed during the process. From H1, the market failed to create a higher high than H, signaling that the bulls are taking a rest. Yet, we still do not have any confirmation about a downtrend. Remember a minimum condition for a downtrend to form is the creation of at least two lower highs and one lower low. In this example, if we see H as the first high and H1 as the first low in a downtrend, then we are lacking one lower low and one lower high.

Once again, let's take a look at the yellow area which illustrates the bearish engulfing pattern on the daily chart. You can see how the engulfing candlestick and even a few following candles constantly failed to break the X line - a horizontal line drawn from H1. This indicates that the market structure still remained unchanged, i.e the uptrend still prevailed at least until the close of the daily engulfing pattern. In other words, the selling pressure was not strong enough to win against the bulls' force. When we observe the 4-hour chart, it is obvious that the above-mentioned engulfing candlestick did not carry in it any evidence of a reversal in connection with market structure. Put differently, it also failed to meet the third condition of a reversal.

If you are not careful in analyzing this candlestick pattern, you may feel something of a betray when a considered profitable pattern failed to work. However, once you know that it failed to meet two out of three needed criteria for a reliable function, you will be relaxed watching the candlesticks to move without putting yourself in dangers. In a "probability market", we should be prudent.

Trading any reversal after successfully confirming all three conditions would greatly increase the chances of stacking the odds in your favor. Below is another example of a bullish engulfing pattern present at a key support level failing to start a reversal.

On the daily time frame, things might be ideal for a reversal to the upside...

However, if you had entered a buy entry right after the highlighted bar, you would have encountered a loss. Let's see what happened on the 4-hour chart below.

Notice that the daily bullish engulfing pattern is comprised of a few 4-hour candlesticks which are in the yellow box.

Still basing on the above method of analyzing the market, we all see the engulfing bar was located in a key support zone, which satisfies the first criterion of a reversal.

As can be seen, the market was in a clear downtrend from A to F, forming lower highs and lower lows. Then, the bullish engulfing bar tried to break the dominant trend by preventing the market from forming a lower low. Unfortunately, it failed to close above E – the newest lower high at that time. Such failure indicated that no change in the market structure was made, thus any ideas of buying the currency pair should be removed. You can see how the market continued its strong downtrend and form a lower low at H. An uptrend had not been formed till several 4-hour candlesticks later. Once again, the second and third criteria of a reversal were not satisfied. Trading right after the bullish engulfing bar would put you in great dangers.

Principle 2: Do not join a reversal trade until the overall market trend/structure has been successfully broken/ changed.

Let's see when and how we could join the market in this situation.

Still on the downtrend, the market continued to make a lower high at I. The problem with the downtrend initiated when the market failed to create a lower low at J. This tells us that, upon touching a strong support zone, the sellers were encountering a strong opposing force from the bulls. They then lost the battle at J, pushing prices higher. Should you be in a position like this, be prepared for a confirmed buy signal.

The market's effort to touch a key support level at J could also be seen as a retest before a strong upward trend. Trading on retests has always been my indispensable principle in every trade.

On analyzing any market structure, for example from a downtrend to an uptrend, the break of the newest high plays a very important part on whether we should enter a trade or not. In this case, notice how the prices strongly broke the X1 level from J, meaning that the nearest/ newest high during a downtrend was broken. And if you were patient enough, such break served to form a higher high at K. There we have it. Notice that after the market created another low at L, it were now having two higher lows (J and L) and one higher high (K), which meets the minimum conditions of an uptrend. A change in the market structure was confirmed by L, which is also the ideal entry price in this case. And here is the interesting point.

Here are the two core reasons I would place an order at L for a high chance of winning.

- Always trade on a retest. Do not be seduced by the market to enter a buy order when the market is present by a very long bull bar or enter a sell order in case of a long bear bar. As I mentioned in previous part, let's connect the price with a ball and you will get the explanation. Imagine how a ball quickly bounces back after strongly hitting the floor. And this is how prices work. Prices need a strong base for any strong advance or drop. Before a rally or plummet, just look for a correction of the overall trend. Technically speaking, it is when buyers and sellers are recharging energy for an imminent powerful move.

- When a support level is broken, it is likely to turn into a resistance level, and vice versa. Let's see how the X2 line played as a strong resistance area in case of E and G highs. After being broken, it played as a support area and prices tended to make retests upon the X2 level. Do not join any trade without a retest. What is the worst outcome of this rule? Missing a trade, that's it.

In fact, there is no need to worry if you know there are unlimited opportunities ahead.

And most importantly, my capital is safely protected by trading this way.

On coming back to the daily time frame, the break of X1 line was clearly illustrated by the second engulfing bar. A strong upward trend was followed by that candlestick.

Let's take a look at another example regarding the GBP/CAD currency pair, and see why the engulfing bar failed to forecast a reversal in the market.

On the daily time frame, an engulfing bar appeared at a key resistance area. However, it failed to trigger a strong enough selling force to pull the price to the below right away. Put differently, if you had placed a sell trade right after the engulfing pattern, your order would have hit the stop loss level. With the same way of explanation as in the previous examples, let's see what happened in the 4-hour chart time frame.

From the 4-hour chart, an uptrend had been prevailing before the bearish engulfing pattern appeared (the daily engulfing pattern is comprised of a few 4-hour candlesticks in the yellow box). It is clear that the engulfing pattern only served to create a new higher low during the overall uptrend. Hence, no reliable bearish signal was present at that moment, and it was best to stay on the sideline.

On looking further in the chart, let's see how the market continued to make a higher high and a higher low at H and I respectively. Yet, the failure to create another higher high at J released the first signal for a downward move.

Now, we have I as the newest/nearest low during the uptrend. From this, I draw a horizontal line, making the X1 line as in the picture. Notice that from J, the market tried two more times to push prices higher but it failed, again and again, forming a top at K. This was when the sellers gathered and battled with the bulls' force which was becoming weaker and weaker. The sellers then won the battle and pulled prices below the X1 line, breaking the nearest low in the uptrend. A new low was formed at L and this was when you should be prepared for a sell signal.

If you still remember a simple characteristic of a downtrend – the creation of at least two lower highs and one lower low – then you will see the importance of M's appearance. It was when the downtrend was confirmed and we had two lower highs (K and M) and one lower low (L). M was what we need to look for an entry price. In fact, it was better if M could touch the X1 line as a retest of the new resistance. Yet, in the picture, the bears seemed so powerful that they prevented the bulls from reaching the level. You can see how strong the downtrend was after the formation of M as the second lower high.

Now, let's stop for a minute for the clarification of MARKET STRUCTURE.

While we can easily identify support/resistance zones on the chart, a correct identification of a change in *market structure* is not a simple task at all. In the above examples, I just identify an uptrend or a downtrend based on one basic characteristic. In fact, it is an effective way of explaining the malfunctions of candlestick patterns. Yet, a reliable confirmation of a market structure's break should be based on specific components, which will, in turn, help to determine appropriate entry and stop levels.

As market structure is a concept that has been mentioned in a trading material for the first time here, let me break it down into smaller criteria for you to grasp and best apply in your trading.

Market Structure – Uptrend To Downtrend

To begin with, a reliable confirmation of a change from an uptrend to a downtrend must include:

- Firstly, the market fails to create a higher high. This (not any other criterion) should be the very first evidence on signaling the tiredness of buyers on pushing the price higher.
- Prices break the last low in the initial uptrend.
- The market successfully creates two lower highs in the new downtrend, and the second high must not be higher than the last low in the previous uptrend.

To avoid any obscurity, let's take a look at an ideal market structure's change from an uptrend to a downtrend:

From the example, we can see:

Firstly, the market fails to create a higher high than A. In fact, C could be at a same or lower price than A. It would be preferred if C is located lower than A.

Secondly, prices break the X line, which is drawn from the last low in the uptrend (B), creating a lower low at D.

Last but not least, the market successfully creates two lower highs at C and E, in which E is not higher than B.

Now, let's come up with a popular false pattern that you should watch out for:

In this example, the third criterion is not satisfied. Although the market forms two lower lows than A (at C and E), the second lower high (E) is higher than the last low during the uptrend (B). This may pave the way for another retest at F before an advance. In these cases, it is advisable to stay on the sideline and watch for other reliable market signals.

Market Structure - Downtrend To Uptrend

Similarly, for a reliable change from a downtrend to an uptrend to be confirmed, three following criteria must be met:

- Firstly, the market fails to create a lower low. This (not any other criterion) should be the very first evidence on signaling a tiredness of sellers on dragging the price lower.
- Prices break the last high during the initial downtrend.

- The market successfully creates two higher lows in the new uptrend, and the second low must not be lower than the last high of the previous downtrend.

Although these three signals are opposite to ones when we consider a change from an uptrend to a downtrend, they are all based on the same principle. Thus, for a quick reference, let me call these three above bullet points "*3MS principles*". Later, when I mention about "3MS principles", just understand that I am referring to three conditions for a market structure's change, either from up to down or vice versa.

Now, let's see how an ideal market structure's change from a downtrend to an uptrend looks like:

From the picture:

Firstly, the market fails to create a lower low than A. In fact, C could be at a same or higher price than A. It would be ideal if C is located a little bit higher than A as in the picture.

Secondly, prices break the last high during the previous downtrend (B), forming a higher high at D.

Last but not least, the market successfully creates two higher lows at C and E, in which E is not lower than B.

Similar to the previous examples, you should be careful when the 3MS principles are not fully satisfied, especially the last criterion. Let's take a look at the below picture:

In this example, problems arise. Although the market forms two higher lows than A (at C and E), the second higher low (E) is lower than the last high during the uptrend (B). This may pave the way for another retest at F before a plummet. In these cases, it is better not enter any trade and to wait for more market signals.

For me, I always trade when there are all three 3M principles present in the chart. This is not to refute a fact that sometimes, we just need two or even one out of the three pieces of evidence for a successful trade. Yet, as I always state, we should be prudent in the Forex market. The more signals we gain for our trades, the better we are at stacking the odds in our favor. I will illustrate this point later in this book.

Coming back to market analysis, I often suggest that the more factors you collect in proving your setups, the more chances of success you will have. In many cases, you can analyze market structure in connection with a trend line, which is, in my opinion, a very powerful method for determining potential market movements.

Let's come up with another example regarding USD/CAD pair.

In this example, we have two daily bearish engulfing patterns not far away from each other. However, just one of them works.

It is ideal you combine with a trend line to see how strong the bearish signal was regarding the second engulfing pattern. Let's take a look at the 4-hour chart time frame, where I often use to determine entry points.

Here it is. Please be noted that the two yellow boxes indicate two daily engulfing bars. First, by using market structure analysis, you can easily explain the first one's failure to drag prices to the below price area, as well as how the second one provided an apparent evidence of selling force dominance.

While the two engulfing patterns are locating at a key resistance area, their voices on telling about market structure's change are different. On applying 3MS principles, it is clear that the first engulfing bar failed to meet all three criteria of a reliable change. Put differently, at the time of the first bar's presence, all three characteristics of the 3MS principles were not met, which accounts for its failure to work that time.

On analyzing market structure's change in the second engulfing bar, we can see it *strongly broke the last low* during the uptrend (D) and then *formed two lower highs* (A and B) in which the second low (B) was located at a lower level than the last low in the uptrend (D). The highest peak during the prior uptrend played as the highest top during the following downtrend. The 3MS principles are fully completed (though the *failure to create a higher high* (forming a top at A) came later than expected).

Moreover, you could see how the second engulfing pattern (the second yellow box) was obviously present during the break of X1 line. This means that the bar itself carried one component of the market structure's break.

All of these account for the reason behind this bar's function on market reversal's angle.

Moreover, by drawing an upward trend line, it is even clearer the first engulfing pattern failed to break the trend line on the 4-hour chart. Conversely, the second engulfing pattern indicated a much stronger selling pressure, breaking the trend line and pulling the price to the below area.

In short, the market structure clearly tells us the correlation between bulls and bears, which side is stronger. Ignoring this may mislead you and result in unexpected losses. In the Forex market, nothing is 100% certain. Hence, the more criteria you have gained through technical analysis, the higher chance you stand on winning trades. This is how you put the odds in your favor.

Chapter 11 Psychology Of Forex Trading

Psychology and trading, most people might think that these factors don't relate to one another. Well, it very well does. As I mentioned earlier, most trading mistakes occur because the traders don't understand the importance of trading psychology. However, most traders don't trade successfully, mainly because of emotional problems. Especially, naïve traders don't handle emotions well, so they don't remain in the market for long. But, it is not something good which is why educating naïve traders is important. Even before they enter the market, it is important to spend the time to learn the market. However, the most common issue with trading is fear. But, fear is commonly seen when the trader moves into the live trading account. But, initially, the temptation is often found in naïve traders. When they enter the market, they enter with the thought of trading as much as possible to make money. Hence, this thought will not let them achieve what they actually should achieve. Therefore, when a trader is tempted to trade, he or she may trade even without analyzing or anticipating the trades.

However, as mentioned fear can also create a lot of issues in a trader's journey. Many traders give up trading completely because of fear. But, the fight or flight reaction is a human thing, that is commonly seen in traders. But actually, this reaction cannot be changed that easily, but of course, traders can handle this reaction wisely. If you study trading psychology, things will become simpler when trading the Forex market. Anyway, when you fear to trade, it will impact your trading behaviors negatively. Most of the time, you will look for a safer method to trade and, perhaps, it is not possible to find safer trading methods in the Forex market.

As you already know, the Forex market involves a lot of risks, so as traders, you must learn to handle them carefully. For example, when you enter into a trade, your instincts point out the chances of losing and you will eventually exit from the trade, and it might have been a profitable trade. So see, your mind has a direct connection to the way you trade.

Even if you have a defined plan, you can still steer away from trading because the power of psychology is immense. You might even become anxious and consider short-term positions because you are afraid to enter into long-term positions even if they seem profitable. Well, yes, fear, greed, and all the other emotions can cause a lot of problems to your trading journey. Hence, you must understand trading psychology. If you do, you will be able to assist those emotions wisely and handle trading successfully. Normally, if you overcome fear, it will be beneficial to your trading journey as well as life.

Typically, traders don't fear the market when they are preparing to enter into a trade, but when the market opens, their emotions play the role. As humans, you can never get rid of emotions because it is a part of humankind. But, you can always learn the methods to control your emotions when excitement is a dangerous emotion when trading the Forex market. When you are excited, you might make mistakes when entering a trade or anticipating market movements. Thus, when you are trading, you have to try to keep your emotions neutral.

Most traders succumb to accept that they are making trading mistakes that are related to psychology. But normally, when people can't accept, denial is the first reaction. Over time, they tend to accept the truth. Just like that, even the naïve traders will learn to accept the truth. However, Forex trading is not only about trading system and strategies. You must accept that mindset is an important part of Forex trading. The way you anticipate the Forex market has a lot to do with trading. Also, only if you understand the trades will you be able to enter into it. Thus, a trader's mindset has a lot to do with trading.

If you look at certain websites that advertise robotic trading systems, you might find trading psychology as an absurd thing. But, remember, those trading systems will not provide benefits as they portray. Nothing is as best as trading manually. You must use your knowledge and skills to trade the market; only then will you be able to trade successfully. Also, those websites are doing their duty to market their product, and if you rely on them and purchase it, you might have to pay them for using their product. Hence, when you come across something like this, make sure to think logically. As a beginner, you must try to settle for a simple yet effective strategy, so that you will be able to trade peacefully.

Anyway, why do you think most naïve traders struggle to make money? You might have seen many people who fail in trading the Forex market. Well, there are many reasons why traders fail, but the major reason is the ones who enter the Forex market don't really know the market. A higher percentage of traders enter into the Forex market by believing the fabricated ads. And it makes them set unrealistic goals. Eventually, they struggle to meet those unrealistic goals and end up quitting trading. But the worst part is that there are traders who quit their day job after they enter the Forex market. Well, it is not a wise move because they must test to check whether trading works for them. Or some other traders believe trading is easy money and no matter how many times I repeat it, some people still believe it is possible. These thoughts create tension and stress, so eventually, the trader becomes emotionally unstable. Thus, when traders trade with an emotionally unstable mindset, they lose money.

So, how can a trader develop a trading mindset? If you want to develop a trading mindset, you need to do your part. It is important to put the required effort to accomplish what you are looking for. Well, you can't build a trading mindset that quickly because you have to learn and accept the Forex market as it is. If you try to deny facts about the Forex market, you will not be able to create a trading mindset.

You must start developing your trading mindset by handling the risks in trading. First of all, understand that risk management isn't for one trade, preferably it is applicable for all the trades that you enter into. You must make sure to calculate the risk for each trade before you enter into it. When you are managing risks, certain emotions might try to confuse you, but you must not let it happen. Once you start handling your emotions wisely, you will be able to manage trades also. However, the simplest way to control emotion when managing risks is to risk ONLY the amount that you can lose. You must create a mindset that enters into a trade while knowing the probability of losing trade. If you follow this, you will be able to remain in the trading world for a long time. But, it takes practice and patience to create a trading mindset that accepts losses. Also, you must master your trading edge. No matter what trading strategy you are using, you must know it completely to trade successfully.

And, remember, overtrading will never create profits. Instead, overtrading will blow all your hard-earned money. You must trade only when you actually see a profit signal. Don't try to trade just because you feel like trading. Or don't try to guess trade because that doesn't work in Forex trading. If you overtrade, it can be challenging to stop, and you'll become an emotional trader.

If you want to build a trading mindset, you must have an organized mindset. So, basically, when you have an organized mindset, you will think about the trading plan, journal, and much more. You must accept the fact that Forex trading is a business. Hence, don't try to gamble in the market. When you are making trading decisions, you must remain calm and steady; only then will you be able to think clearly.

But then, after you build a trading mindset, you must not let emotions play their role. However, the most common emotions that you must avoid are:

Euphoria

You might argue that euphoria is good, yes, it is good. But when it is related to the Forex market, it becomes dangerous. For example, if a trader wins a few profitable traders, he or she might become confident when trading the next trade. Well, it is good to feel confident when entering the next trade, but feeling overly confident is not a good thing. When traders become overly confident, they don't watch or study the market as they did before.

The consecutive profitable trades should not get into your mind and increase the level of confidence. When trading Forex if you are overconfident, you will not be able to accept the loss if the trade doesn't react the way you wanted. Hence, it is better to remain calm even if you make profits continuously.

Fear

Most traders who enter the market with no knowledge about trading tend to fear the market. Also, some traders might fear because they cannot effectively trade using any specific strategy. However, usually, when a trader continuously experiences losses, he or she may tend to fear to trade. Perhaps, it is understandable because losing hard-earned money isn't easy. But, you can avoid the mistake of risking more than the amount that you are comfortable with. Most naïve traders don't follow this rule even if we keep repeating it. If fear persists, you will not be able to trade better trades or become successful. It has the power to keep you away from good trades as well. Hence, try to overcome fear by limiting the amount you risk in trading. For the naïve traders, start your journey on a demo account without directly entering the live account. If you do so, you'll be able to learn to control emotions.

Greed

You might have heard that people say only bulls and bears make money, but pigs get slaughtered. If you don't understand what it means, it means greed. If you are greedy, you will not be able to make money in the market. Instead, you will be kicked out of the market. Mostly, traders become greedy when they don't have self-discipline. Most traders make quick decisions when the market shows profitable trade signals, but it is not recommended. Instead, you must be calm and collected. Take some time to understand the market, focus on the risk ratio, set a plan, and then enter into the trade. Also, remember, if you are risking more than what you are ready to lose, it apparently shows your level of greed to make money. Thus, you must overcome greed if you don't want to lose your account.

Revenge

This is one of the funny behaviors of traders because what is the point in revenging the market? For the Forex market, you are just one amongst the millions, and it doesn't make sense. However, if you are trying to revenge trade just because you lost a few trades, remember, this might lead to further losses. When you are emotional, you will not be able to make wise decisions. Hence, you must wait for some time until your mind is stable and ready to trade.

So, when learning the psychology of trading, you might find it exciting. But, success can decide when you take these things into practice. You don't have to try these tips and ideas on the live account, instead use the demo account. The Forex market is one of the best markets because it has provided solutions for almost all the issues. So, as traders, if you solve your personal trading issues, you will be able to become a successful trader. But how to succeed in trading?

Chapter 12 Tips For Success

Keep the risk in mind

Before you go ahead and make the decision to ultimately pull the trigger on any potential currency trade you are currently considering, the first thing you are going to want to go ahead and make sure that you know how likely you are to get your money back as well as actually turn a profit. This is why it is always so important to analyze the data that you gather as there is no other way of determining the mood the market is in which means essentially going into a trade just to gamble, and there are better ways to gamble than through the forex market. Additionally, you will want to know when to go ahead and cut your losses and having a clear idea of the overall level of risk will make this easier to determine as well.

With a clear idea of what sort of risk is going to be required for the trade in question, you will then have more tools at your disposal when it comes time to actually mitigate the risk that you have found, or at least to decrease it as much as possible. Ensuring that the odds of actually turning a profit are in your favor means setting a tight stop loss and not letting your emotions get in the way in the heat of the moment. The point that you start a trade and the point that you set your stop loss at can be considered the maximum amount of risk you are accepting for a given trade.

It is important to always determine the acceptable amount of risk you can handle before you actually make the trade, when your emotions are of a nominal concern. If you wait to set a stop loss until after the trade is already in progress, then you run the risk of letting your emotions cloud your better judgement and losing profits in the process. If you feel the need to change your stop loss coming on then you are going to want to take a moment and consider exactly what it is you are thinking about doing and if it is something that you would consider if you were just getting in at that moment. With a few moment's consideration, your answer should be clear.

To keep your emotions from getting the better of you, prior to going into each trade you are going to want to keep in mind the point that you will always get out when you are happy with your profits, no matter what. When it comes to maximizing your profits, a stopping point is just as important as a good stop loss point. You may be tempted to stay in as long as possible in an effort to squeeze the most profit out of a good trade as possible, but this will lose you more than it will make you in the long run, guaranteed. Instead, the right choice is to cash out half of your holdings and then pick a new point further up so that you protect your profits while also maximizing them.

Finally, regardless of how much of a sure thing a specific trade may appear to be, you need to get in the habit of never investing more than you can afford to lose in a single trade. This means that if you start with $5,000 that you can invest in the forex market then you never want any single trade to cost you more than $100. This is what is known as the 2 percent rule and it is crucial to remaining financially solvent while investing in forex, especially when you are just starting out. While you will likely come up against moments where you want nothing more than to buck this trend, especially when you are riding high on a quality pair, sticking with it is what separates successful forex traders from amateurs. If you can't afford to lose it, don't put it in the pot, it is as simple as that.

Trade with the right mindset

If you ever hope to stick around the market long enough to think of yourself as an expert trader, there are several skills you are going to need to become very adept at using. First and foremost, this means always trading with a cool head, no matter what. When you are trading, your goal should be to be as emotionless and robotic as possible. The only thing that matters when you are trading is the numbers and if you worry about anything else while doing so, you are doing it wrong. Trading in the forex market successfully often means having the ability to make split second decisions, something that just can't be done if you let your emotions get in the way.

Understanding the fact that your emotions are only getting in the way and acting on that fact are two extremely different things. The first emotion that you are going to need to focus on banishing is anger. It can be easy to get angry when a trade that appears as though it is going to be a sure thing suddenly turns sideways, but a more effective use of that time is to instead immediately do what is required to minimize the losses, rather than standing there yelling at them. Aside from anger, the most common emotion that you are likely to come across is going to be fear. It can be easy to become afraid, especially if you broke the 2 percent rule and invested too heavily in a single pair; that doesn't mean it is productive, however, and indeed it can be even more dangerous than anger as it can be paralyzing as well. To prevent this from happening you will need to train yourself to push the emotion aside and act on the facts if you ever hope to find real success in the forex market.

Chapter 13 FAQs On Forex Trading

It is obvious that you will have a few questions pop up when you take up a new topic. In this chapter, we will look at some of the most common questions that get asked on the topic of forex trading and answer them to help you understand it better.

Is The Forex Trade Lucrative?

Yes. Forex trading is a lucrative business. You will have the chance to make a lot of money if you understand how exactly to play. We looked at the basic concepts and strategies that you need to employ when you choose the currencies to trade in. Once you choose the best pair, you can easily make a lot of money from it. You have to remain alert and attentive, and that will help you in a big way. You can make thousands of dollars a year by indulging in forex trading.

Should I Be Commerce Literate For It?

No. You don't necessarily have to be commerce literate for it. You also don't have to have any relevant experience in the stock market in order to invest in forex trading. You will be able to start from scratch and make it big in the world of currency investments. The currency market welcomes everyone with open arms and does not really discriminate. It will not know who is a beginner and who is an expert and will treat everyone the same way. So don't think of your lack of knowledge or experience as a drawback to trade in the stock market.

What About Bid/ Ask, Spread, Etc.?

Bid/ask and spread are all terminologies that you should acquaint yourself with before you start investing. These are common terms that are used across all stock market trades and are not unique to just forex trade. Once you understand what these terms stand for you can easily start trading in forex. You can go through a glossary of all these terms and understand each carefully.

How Much Money Should I Invest?

That is completely up to you. When you open an account to trade in forex, the company might ask you to deposit a certain sum. This sum can be $100 or $250 depending on the company. You don't have to use up all of the amount to invest and can allow some of it to remain back in the account. You might have to maintain a certain minimum amount which cannot be used or invested and will make for a buffer in case you are unable to pay for any of the investments that you have already made. There are people who use as less as $10 to make thousands of dollars of profit.

Can I Trade On My Own?

Yes. You can independently trade in the forex market. You don't have to rely on others to do it for you. It follows a very simple process where you type in the name of the currencies and also type in the amount. Once it is approved, you will be given your currency. You then hold it until you wish to sell it again. You can continue with this process for as long as you like. There is no limit on how much you can buy and sell. If at the very beginning you find it tough to indulge in this process then you can take the help of an expert to get started with it.

Can I Trade Over The Phone?

Yes. You can trade over the phone. You need to call your broker and ask him to buy you the certain currencies. You can also have the currency buying software installed on your phone and use it to buy and sell your currencies.

It is really simple and will help you trade in currencies on the go.

Why Do The Currency Prices Fluctuate?

There are many factors that contribute towards the fluctuation in the currency prices. There are economic and political causes that affect the prices and cause it to change. There are also other geographic and business-related causes that can cause the currency prices to vary. There is just no telling what will end up influencing the prices of the currencies and will entirely depend on the current events.

Can I Have My Account Funded?

Yes. You can have your account funded by someone else. They will have to directly add the money to your account in order for you to invest it. But you have to show evidence that they have willfully added in the money into your account for you to use in forex. There is no limit on the amount that can be transferred to your account.

Can I Withdraw All Profits?

Yes. You can withdraw the entire amount that you get as profit from your forex trade. But you might have to leave behind a certain amount that is seen as the minimum balance that needs to be maintained. You have to leave that much behind and ensure that you don't invite any unnecessary fines. Some companies might not even have this minimum balance scheme, and you can easily withdraw all the money at once.

Will I Get Possession Of The Foreign Currencies?

Yes and no. It depends on the time that you wish to hold the currency. If the time exceeds the 5-day limit, then you might have to take possession of the currency. If you are indulging in intra-day trading, then you will not have to take physical possession of it.

These form the different FAQs that get asked on the topic and hope you had yours answered successfully.

Conclusion

Forex trading is not for everyone. You should never trade what you cannot afford to lose. In addition, you should be committed to keeping your emotions out of your trading decisions while making smart decisions based on facts.

If Forex trading is for you, then it is important to set realistic expectations. Even the very best traders like Warren Buffet only increased their portfolio by 20 percent a year while most hedge fund managers are thrilled to grow their portfolios by 10 percent a year.

There are many approaches to Forex trading. Your personality, your available time and your ability to read market indicators all play important factors in determining the best approach for you. Regardless of your approach, however, it is important to think before you trade as statistics show that the best way to lose money in Forex trading is to trade too often.

www.ingramcontent.com/pod-product-compliance
Lightning Source LLC
Chambersburg PA
CBHW070340220526
45467CB00001B/189